More
Reflections
for
Managers

More Reflections for Managers

Bruce N. Hyland
Merle J. Yost

McGraw-Hill, Inc.

New York   San Francisco   Washington, D.C.   Auckland   Bogotá
Caracas   Lisbon   London   Madrid   Mexico City   Milan
Montreal   New Delhi   San Juan   Singapore
Sydney   Tokyo   Toronto

Library of Congress Cataloging-in-Publication Data

Hyland, Bruce.
    More reflections for managers / Bruce N. Hyland, Merle J. Yost.
        p.   cm.
    Previous ed. published under title: Reflections for managers.
    ISBN 0-07-031785-2
    1. Industrial management . 2. Psychology, Industrial. I. Yost,
Merle J.. II. Hyland, Bruce N. Reflections for managers.
III. Title.
HD31.H95   1995   95-33419
658—dc20   CIP

McGraw-Hill

*A Division of The **McGraw·Hill** Companies*

1 2 3 4 5 6 7 8 9 0   DOC/DOC 9 0 0 9 8 7 6 5

ISBN 0-07-031785-2

The sponsoring editor for this book was Philip Ruppel, the editing supervisor was Bernard Onken, and the production supervisor was Suzanne Rapcavage. It was set in Palatino by Terry Leaden of McGraw-Hill's Professional Book Group Unit.

Printed and bound by R. R. Donnelley & Sons Company.

 This book is printed on recycled, acid-free paper containing a minimum of 50% recycled, de-inked fiber.

*To the people who accept
the enormous responsibility of
making a difference in other
people's lives.*

*And to the people who have
made an enormous difference
in our lives.*

Contents

Working with People

Increasing Productivity

Understanding and Motivating the Team

Making Things Work

·Creativity and Innovation

Getting the Big Picture

Preface

In this second book in the Reflections for Managers Series, we invite you to join us as we continue our exploration of management. We call this our journey because we believe that we, even as the authors, must join you as we explore ourselves, our organizations, and our society in search of better and better ways to work together.

Being a manager is alternately exciting, depressing, challenging, boring, fun, scary, fulfilling, and lonely. It is, at the least, a very enlivening career. Whether you've found your way here by plan (attending the best MBA schools) or by accident (being promoted because you were a good worker), your destiny is the same.

You are the person your employees look to for guidance and the person your organization looks to in order to make it a success. How you respond to that challenge and responsibility will determine your destiny.

In our management, consulting, and counseling careers we have experienced every one of these emotions. We've felt the weight of responsibility, the sting of failure, the joy of seeing individuals and teams come alive, and the ultimate thrill of success. In experiencing these we learned better ways to handle the responsibility which was entrusted to us.

We also continue to ask executives, managers, supervisors, and employees for their insights. We would certainly not be so arrogant as to believe that we have all the answers. By listening, carrying on an exploratory dialogue, and sharing our insights, we find ways to improve our managerial skill. *More Reflections* brings you the latest insights we have gathered as we continue this adventure.

This time we offer several more themes in management: Professionalism; "People" Development; Working with People; Increasing Productivity; Understanding and Motivating the Team; Making It Work; Creativity and Innovation; The Big Picture; and Managers Are Human, Too.

This is a journey that can be a lot of fun. We invite you to explore that part of the journey with us as well. If you spend a career in management and retire without saying that it was fun, then you got lost along the way. Perhaps in some small way this book will show you how to have fun and enjoy your work. We hope so.

Come now and explore with us the continuing journey of management.

Bruce N. Hyland
Merle J. Yost

The Fine Art of Being a Professional

1
ACCEPT YOUR RESPONSIBILITY

You're the boss. You are ultimately responsible. You cannot abdicate that. When you accept your responsibility, you claim your power and earn people's respect.

In More Depth

To accept your responsibility might sound redundant. After all, you are the boss and you are responsible, right? So far so good, but this rule goes further. To accept your responsibility means to fully accept it: no blaming, no passing the buck; being committed to do whatever it takes to make sure the job gets done, and actually accepting the reality that it is up to you. It is the very act of fully accepting responsibility that gives you great power.

You have certain influence by the mere fact of being the formal boss. Don't assume that the title conveys full power. You earn full power when you behave professionally in a manner that says you have not only formal power but also personal power, because you know in your bones that you accept your responsibility. Somehow, some way, that message comes across to employees.

Certainly you can delegate your power, and should. Ultimately, however, you must accept responsibility. By being fully responsible and yet sharing power with those whom you assign responsibility, you earn the respect and sometimes the admiration of the people who work for and with you.

The Idea in Action

Pamela was director of marketing for an international architectural firm. She had a habit of not accepting full responsibility for her division. When problems arose, she would frequently find reasons that were "not my fault." She would point to the economy, lack of support from the tech team, the foul-up by an employee, or the activities of the competition.

Word got around that she was not a responsible leader. Pamela wasn't a bad person. She simply did not accept full responsibility for her position or her professional behavior.

One day the vice president told her he was unhappy with this pattern. She initially tried the same old behavior, blaming everything and everybody. "Stop," he said. "Certainly there are things that happen, but all that is your responsibility to deal with. I don't expect you to be able to control some things; but I do expect you to be responsible enough to see it as a part of your job to deal with. Stop blaming."

She was very upset and thought of quitting. Fortunately, she didn't. Instead, she accepted her responsibility, faced the issues squarely, and stopped the blaming.

For Reflection

How do you send signals to your employees that you accept responsibility for your functional area?

In what way do you demonstrate personal and professional responsibility?

What area of your job do you have trouble taking responsibility for?

2
LEARN FROM OTHERS

Great ideas are as close as the people around you. There are good ideas every-where. Learn from them. Learn from competitors, employees, colleagues, ene-mies, friends, teachers, mentors, children, and people on the street.

In More Depth

Adopt an attitude that everyone has something to teach you. With that attitude, you will be amazed to discover just how true it is. We tend to think that we learn primarily from our professors, our bosses, or "outside experts." That's true. But there are many others who may teach us just as much.

The first step in learning from others is to be open to learning, to admit that we do not already have the answers. Then we must bring some focus to learning. For example, when we're just having a con-versation to be polite or pleasant, we can ask for another person's per-spective on something that interests us. We must also listen with the intention of learning. This means that we must pay attention to what someone is telling us, to see what value lies there.

Yes, there are gold mines all around you. You simply must decide to go exploring and mine them.

The Idea in Action

Emily was the creative director of an advertising agency. For years the agency had won awards for advertising. Then, it just seemed to lose its vitality and magic.

Emily was very distressed. The creative types still did good work, but their pool of ideas seemed to dry up. They found themselves recycling older ideas in new ways. Emily tried motivational speeches, threatening speeches, beach parties, brainstorming exercises, and more. Nothing seemed to work. They were in a rut, and she knew it.

At the end of the day Emily hailed a cab. The cabby asked her how the job was going. She replied, "Awful." We're in a rut and I don't have any new ideas." He smiled. "So you need new ideas? Just ask me. I've got lots of ideas." She was annoyed at his flippancy. "OK, what's a new idea for selling a bar of soap?" He smiled again. "Forget talking about how clean it makes you; sell it for how much fun you can have in the shower with it. My wife and I enjoy our soap," he said with a wink.

She knew that she had found her answer. She had stopped learning from people. She and her staff had fallen prey to believing that they were the only ones with ideas. Emily and her team vowed to learn from others. They asked, listened, observed, and generally opened themselves up to continuous learning.

Today the awards are back.

For Reflection

How do you learn from others?
What were the two best ideas you got from someone last week?
What do you think stops people from learning from others?

3
DEVELOP REAL POWER

Real power comes when people willingly help you and the organization achieve your goals. In reality, power is an illusion—it must be given, not demanded.

In More Depth

Power is one of those concepts that we all think we understand, yet find difficult to define. That's because power is more than just being named the boss. Real power is much more difficult to attain and carries with it an enormous responsibility. To become a great manager, it is important to develop real power.

When people see you as powerful, they want to have you manage and lead them. You are vested with a power which supersedes any formal authority. Just imagine the difference. Think of someone you have enjoyed working for and went that extra mile to help. You gave that person your best. Then think of someone you have worked for and did not like. Did you go the extra mile for that person? Did he or she get your best? That's the difference between formal power and real power.

When your employees respect your use of power, and you use it fairly and with good intentions, you will be rewarded with the real thing. They will respect you and go that extra mile.

The Idea in Action

Mona was elected president of the local PTA. Mona called the board members together and gave them their objectives for the year. She asked that they report to her every month and to consult her before they made any decisions. Several were quite annoyed with her authoritarian approach.

Behind her back, the board members began talking. "Power sure has gone to her head! She used to be helpful and anxious to work with us, but now that she is president she rules like a tyrant." As a result, they engaged in no progressive work, since they "were not given the authority by Madame President" (as they had taken to calling her).

When Mona thought about running for another term, she polled each board member. She thought they were 100 percent with her. To her surprise, she found that almost no one wanted her to run. She was hurt and angry. She cornered the board members and demanded to know why.

"If you must know, you hog all the power. You're obsessed with power," they told her.

Mona was shocked. She had the best of intentions, but she had to admit that power had gone to her head. She decided to forget about reelection and mend her ways. The board members were so impressed that by the next month they were saying she should run again.

For Reflection

How do you define and use power?

What excuses have you heard from other managers for not sharing power?

How would your organization respond if power were given to people—the power, responsibility, and authority to achieve?

4

ACT OPENLY...THERE ARE VERY FEW SECRETS IN AN ORGANIZATION

Pretend your mind and office have glass windows. Act accordingly. People actually know most of what is going on in every organization.

In More Depth

Every organization has its grapevine, gossip group, and informal connections. They all serve to pass information—and the juiciest information is the "secret." It is a currency of status within most organizations.

Act openly, not to avoid getting caught, but to involve people in the organization. Have them become a whole part of the team. Share information and insights so that people can do their jobs better, with more knowledge of how it all fits together. Secrecy builds distrust. When people feel you are hiding something, they begin to trust less and less. Act openly and you will find your life and your job as a manager much easier.

The Idea in Action

Oliver headed the trust department of a banking conglomerate. His department had fiduciary responsibilities and had to maintain discretion and confidentiality for its clients.

Oliver, though, carried the confidentiality notion too far in his management. He did practically everything in secret. He always had "closed-door meetings." He never told anyone what organizational changes were pending. He failed to inform his staff of events in other parts of the bank. He would disappear for hours every day, and no one knew where he went. (Well, no one except Doris, who was his personal secretary. And Doris told only Tony, her trusted friend. Tony then traded that information only with Don, who worked in the mail-sorting area, in exchange for finding out what was in that memo from corporate headquarters.)

The staff made a game of "figuring out what was going on." As time went on, the plots they conceived grew wilder and wilder. Some of these concocted stories made it to the clients, and others got to senior management.

When the word got back to Oliver, he was shocked and embarrassed. He realized that he had fostered much of the problem himself. He called a department meeting. He admitted that he needed to be more open. From that day on, things became more open and Oliver and his team's productivity skyrocketed.

For Reflection

Why do you think some managers try to hide so much?

Have you ever lost respect for or lost trust in one of your managers who acted secretively?

What is one step that you could take to act more openly?

5

THE LEADER GOES FIRST

Everyone waits for someone else to go first. Few people like the risk of being out there alone. Leadership requires it.

In More Depth

Your position requires you to go first. That is the essence of leadership: You step out, you lead. In your position as manager and leader, you need to demonstrate courage and conviction. You do this by taking the risk of going first. People want leadership. That is your job. You are the one who must be willing to take the risk of going into the unknown.

You will need to take the lead in your relationships with people. You must make the first moves—to meet or greet someone, to initiate resolution of a conflict, to face down a troublemaker, to make the first contact with a potential joint partner, to talk with the officials who have an impact over your operation, to deal with troublesome situations which nobody wants to touch. This is leadership.

As a manager and leader, you need to embrace the excitement and exuberance of stepping out and being the first. Jump up and volunteer. Say what you want to say and what the group needs you (as leader) to say. Try something new and show your people that you aren't afraid of trying.

The Idea in Action

Abe was a city manager in the Southwest. Early in his career, he had established a reputation for leadership. Over the past few years he tended to become less of a leader. People said, "Abe used to be the first to try new ways of doing things. He used to take risks, initiate public contact, and seize opportunities. Lately, he just takes the least risky path. We miss the 'old' Abe."

Their observations were true. Several years earlier, Abe had been the first to take a stand on an unpopular issue. Ultimately, his position was vindicated. However, in the process he was politically battered.

Perhaps because of this, Abe stopped going first. He stopped leading and focused on administrative duties. The city, his staff, and the public missed his earlier progressive stance. One day he asked for honest feedback and got it: "Abe, you are a fine man, but you are losing your leadership skill. You have stopped going first. You've stopped taking the initiative. We want you to lead again."

Abe was shocked by the comment. Over the course of the next year, he once again took courageous first steps. He initiated new action for the city. He put forth new ideas. It was the "old" Abe again.

For Reflection

What actions have you demonstrated lately in which you "went first"?
Why do you think many managers and leaders stop going first?
What stops you from going first?

6

MAKE YOUR WORD GOLD

Whenever you make a promise, keep it. Whenever you say no, stand behind it. Whenever you make agreements, live by them.

In More Depth

People who keep their word become the most important members of an organization. People come to rely on and trust that person. They can be counted on. *You* need to be that person in your organization.

Whenever you make a promise, be sure to keep it. When you keep your promises, no matter how much effort it takes, you will be rewarded.

Whenever you say no, stand behind that as well. In a way, a no is also a promise. A good, clean no can be very important in building trust. People feel safest when they know what is expected, what they can and cannot do.

Agreements are also important. Whenever you enter an agreement, live by it. Even if after making the agreement you're not too happy with the deal, you still live by it. In the long run, your integrity will pay off.

This all boils down to an issue of integrity. You need to have the integrity to make your word gold. Integrity comes from your very core. When you keep your word, confidence resonates from your very being. People respond.

The Idea in Action

Victoria was hired as general manager of an entertainment megastore. She knew that she had to gain trust from her employees. She understood the technical side of the business, so there was no question about what needed to be done to run the store. It was in personnel management that she knew she had to pay special attention. She decided on one simple rule: "Make my word gold."

Victoria set out to do that with a vengeance. She was very careful, however, of not overpromising. When she did, she moved mountains to make sure that she came through. After a while, the store employees came to trust and respect her like no manager they had ever had. The teamwork became magical. People followed her example. They started to live up to their word.

Victoria also went to great lengths to carry out all her agreements, even if they weren't formally labeled as promises. On those rare occasions when it was just impossible to do, she would go back to the employee and renegotiate another agreement. The new agreement then became her highest priority. That did not reduce her respect. People understood. Also, she was very good about giving clear yes or no answers. She meant what she said, and people appreciated that.

For Reflection

How do you make your word gold?

When have you gone the extra mile to demonstrate your commitment to your word?

Do you give clear yes or no responses? Do you stand behind them?

7
LEAD BY EXAMPLE

The truth is that you always lead by example. Employees take their cue from you. Your behavior becomes the organizational model. They will emulate you.

In More Depth

Employees reflect their leadership. As human beings, we observe what others do. If these other people hold power, prestige, or influence, we emulate them. We want to be like them. We take our cues from our leaders.

In reality, leading by example is a hard rule. It requires you to be rigorous about your own behavior. It requires you as the manager to be aware of the signals you are sending. People see what you do far more than hear what you say.

As a result, it is vital to lead by example. Live your words. Be congruent with the organization's values, your values, and the behavior and attitudes you expect from your people. Remember, you have no choice. You are already leading by example.

The Idea in Action

Harry started his career as assistant manager for a fast-food outlet. He had difficulty making the transition from employee to manager. He didn't really know what management entailed, and he was given little training or guidance.

Since he was assistant manager, he felt that he was above the rules. He didn't clean up his own work area even though it was a stated rule. When he took breaks (in front of all the employees), he would sit there longer than the allowed time. He'd call in "sick" to take "mental health days" off, later telling his employees about going to the beach or hanging out at the coffee shop.

As it turned out, Harry's employees began ignoring the work rules. They thought, "After all, Harry does it, so it's OK." All this, and more, began to get to Harry. He became angry with his employees. They also had some choice words about him. It went downhill from there.

Harry got fired from his management position, went back to school, and studied management. Harry learned the principle of leading by example. Soon the reason for his failed earlier leadership became abundantly clear. He got another job and became very disciplined about modeling professional behavior. Today he is regional manager.

For Reflection

What examples are you setting for your employees?
What would your employees say if they were asked?
What examples would you like to set for your team players as you lead them?

8

MAKE THE TOUGH DECISIONS

Making tough decisions is part of the management job. That's what you're paid to do. It means that you will not always be liked or popular.

In More Depth

Sometimes you will have to make tough decisions—decisions that may be unpopular or difficult. This is where you become a leader. You will need to take a stand and make a decision on the basis of your best judgment. When you do so, you may find yourself standing alone.

It's the ability and willingness on your part to make these tough decisions that will set you apart as a great manager. Weak managers try to defer, ignore, or shift the decision to someone else. A strong manager will simply make the decision. Certainly, this does not mean that you will make the decision callously. Rather, you will give it your best consideration, examining the pros and cons. You may engage in dialogue with others to get their input. You may want to take a while longer to consider all the ramifications, but ultimately it is your decision.

Making tough decisions just comes with the territory. You will gain respect from your employees. You will also gain self-esteem, knowing that you had the courage to make an important decision that you honestly felt would help the organization.

The Idea in Action

Rob was general manager of a large car dealership. Rob was a respected manager. He had earned that respect, not because of his intelligence or hard work, but because of his willingness to make tough decisions.

One time a friend of Rob's came to work for the dealership. Paul was fun and likable, but he abused his friendship with Rob by coming in late, leaving without telling anyone, cheating "a little" on his expense report, and generally behaving in a less than professional manner.

Rob talked with Paul about his behavior, but he continued to "cross the line," and Rob finally had to fire him. It was a very tough decision. Not only were they friends, but also their families ran in the same social circles. "It was the right thing to do," Rob would reply when questioned. It *was* the right thing to do and everyone, including Paul, knew it—but it didn't make the decision any less difficult.

At his retirement dinner, the employees hailed Rob as a fine manager and a fine man: "He is a true professional who made the tough decisions which allowed the business, his people, and his community to enjoy better lives."

For Reflection
What was the last tough decision you made?
What stops you from making the tough decisions?
How do you view managers who make the tough decisions?

9

THE LEADER SETS THE "TONE" OF THE ORGANIZATION

Set high standards for yourself and your organization.

In More Depth

It is a truism that organizations take on the personality and business tone of their leadership. We could examine the reasons: people hire people like themselves, subordinates try to please the boss, the manager has real power to shape behavior, and so on. That is interesting, but not particularly relevant for our discussion. The real key is that the manager, you, must be responsible for the "tone" you set in the organization.

If your style is dictatorial, you will get direct action, but little dissent (even if it is valid and could help the organization). If your style is open, you will get lots of feedback and information—but will you get things done? If your style is collegial, you will develop colleagues—but will they follow your leadership when necessary?

We don't purport to tell you what your style should be, or even if there *is* a good management style. Rather, we simply point out that your style and the tone you set in the organization will be reflected.

The Idea in Action

Wesley was a young manager of a sales team. He was a very aggressive salesman. As such, he had a great track record for gross sales. He didn't concentrate much on repeat business, but he was so good at closing that he still produced good numbers. Thus, Wesley was promoted.

He immediately called the team together and told them that he wanted to increase sales by 25 percent; therefore, everyone was to call on 25 percent more people. Several salespeople spoke up and said that they couldn't make more calls if they were going to service their existing customers.

Wesley bluntly told them that even though service was nice, it wasn't as important as calling on new prospects. "Just get out there and sell!" he belted. "If it crosses into the gray area when they ask something, it's OK to stretch the truth if you don't lie."

Six months down the road the regional office started getting complaints from customers who were not being visited for follow-up service. The regional manager talked with Wesley. He seemed uninterested in hearing the complaints and became defensive and aggressive. It was clear that Wesley had set the tone for that team.

For Reflection

How would you describe the tone you set for your organization?

How would your team describe the tone you set? (Be honest. It might be the most valuable information you will ever get.)

What tone do you want to set for your team?

10

BE ON TIME

Show up on time for appointments. You will demonstrate commitment, respect, and integrity.

In More Depth

How do you feel when someone keeps you waiting—even if it is your boss? Even if you are "paid the same" whether you're waiting or working? People hate it. People resent it. They *do* get the message: "My time is more important than yours." Translation: "*I* am more important than you."

You are the most powerful when you are committed to something. How do you demonstrate commitment? You take steps to make things happen. You make it a priority in your life. Showing up on time is one way of very visibly demonstrating that commitment. It also calls forth other people's commitment. If you want to feel the impact, turn the situation around. Would you question the commitment of an employee who always showed up to your meetings late? Probably so. Would you be likely to give that employee your best effort when he or she wanted something? Probably not.

Do you try harder for people who respect you? Nearly everyone does. Your employees are no different. Show up on time.

The Idea in Action

Carl was the executive director of a United Way agency. He was a very busy man who frequently attended meetings, gave speeches, and talked with constituents—all in addition to his daily operational duties.

Although excellent at public relations, Carl was less successful at daily operations. He would call a staff meeting for 9:00 a.m. and then arrive around 9:20. The staff started showing up at 9:05, then 9:10, then 9:20, and sometimes later. Carl often had to rush the meeting to make a presentation to the local community organizations. Staffers began to take the meetings for granted. Groups stopped asking him to make presentations.

His secretary covered for him, but secretly hated lying. It became the expectation, and the joke, that he would never be on time. As a result, people started missing meetings with Carl and constituents began requesting that he come to their office instead (so they didn't have to waste their time). Needless to say, even greater disruptions arose in his schedule.

No one ever said that he didn't have integrity. The discontent with Carl was his lack of respect for other people's time.

As a result, respect for him and his organization declined.

For Reflection

How often are you late?
Do you really mean it when you set a time?
Do you apologize when you dishonor people by making them wait?

"People" Development

11

KNOW THE VALUE OF YOUR PEOPLE

That's flesh and blood you're dealing with. People are three-dimensional and are your greatest organizational asset. Find out what lies beneath the surface and you may well uncover a gold mine.

In More Depth

People will make or break your organization. They will make or break your career. Such is the power of people.

When managers truly understand this, they can decide on which side of the table to place their bet. A successful manager will bet on people. People are powerful. Unlike a machine, which has a capacity limited to whatever it was designed for, human potential is unlimited. People can see a new way of doing things. They can bring in the business. They can ease a patient's pain. They can pull together and come up with amazing results.

Like most things which are very valuable, however, people can be fragile. Remember the admonition: handle with care. It's important to take time to get to know and understand your most valuable asset.

Learn the value of your people. Get to know their limits and their potential.

The Idea in Action

Yao was elected to the board of directors for a regional environmental institute. The board was a large, active working group. He was expected to "manage" this board and also have an active role in guiding senior-level operational managers.

Yao didn't have much experience in management, but he did have great people sense. Prior to his election, most people on the board and in senior management were left pretty much on their own. They got things done, but there was no "magic" in their teamwork.

Yao decided to spend time coaching, nurturing, supporting, cajoling, and assisting the board and management. He got to know each one of these people. He found that one board member used to be an accountant, but no one had ever asked for his insight or help on financial matters. Another board member had raised a lot of funds for her church, but was never invited to participate in the fund-raising plan, despite the fact that she had a great interest in it.

Yao knew the value of his people (his colleagues, staff, and volunteers). The other board members took note of his style, as did senior management. During Yao's 2-year tenure as chairman, the organization flourished. People contributed more time and energy (yes, and money). True, Yao didn't know much about management, but he was a great leader of people. He mined for gold in his people, and he found it.

For Reflection

How do you uncover the value in your employees?

What discoveries have you made when you did "mine for gold" among the people on your team?

Do you spend more time maintaining your people or your machines?

12

PROVIDE EDUCATION AND TRAINING

People must know how to do their jobs. To improve performance, you must improve their ability to perform. People can do only as much as they know how to do.

In More Depth

It would be ideal if every employee could and would do everything on the job well. Seldom is that the case. Managers get angry and blame the employees, who in turn see management as mean or incompetent. An employee performs poorly for one of two reasons: either attitude (willingness) or aptitude (ability to do the job).

This is one of the easiest problems in business to solve and it produces one of the greatest payoffs. If there is a magic pill in organizations that solves the worst problem and gives the best payoff, this is it.

Decide exactly what it is you want done. Communicate that to your employees. Assess whether they know how to do it (or how to do it well, for that matter). Then train them in the best way to complete the job. This sounds simple, but it is important. It will produce amazing results. Take the time. Educate and train your people so that they can perform.

The Idea in Action

Macy was a successful retail store manager. She noticed that she had become upset with her employees over the last few years. She thought, "These people just don't seem to be doing their jobs. It's not like it used to be. Worse, I can't seem to find good people who can do the job!"

Macy bemoaned her fate to another seasoned manager who had "seen it all." The manager asked, "Do you think it is because people don't want to do the job or because they don't know how to do the job?"

Macy wanted to answer that people just had a bad attitude, but she knew better. One or two might have a bad attitude, but not to the degree that she was seeing generally in her employees. Besides, if they all just had a bad attitude, that definitely reflected on her hiring process and her management. She concluded that indeed they may not know how to do the job.

She knew the answer to this problem. If people don't know what to do, tell them what to do and show them how to do it. She instituted training classes to cover all the important aspects of her employees' jobs. She invited questions, sometimes even anonymous questions, so that employees wouldn't feel embarrassed about asking something that they "should" have known.

It worked. Productivity jumped 38 percent in the first quarter after the education and training started.

For Reflection

How many of your employees do you "suspect" might not know exactly what they are supposed to do or know how to do it?

What are the most important things that your employees need to know how to do?

What kind of training would produce the biggest results for you? The quickest results?

13

HOLD ON TO TOP TALENT

All you really have is your people. Good employees are hard to find. Great employees are even harder to find. When you have them, hold on to them.

In More Depth

We joke about how "hard it is to find good help these days." It's true. It is very difficult and enormously expensive to advertise, recruit, interview, hire, and train employees. Even after doing all that, we consider ourselves lucky if the employee turns out to be an outstanding one, or even just a good one. With all the time and money expended to get top talent, it is vital that we hold on to our people.

What a pleasure it is to have great employees! They work hard, they make significant contributions to the team, they are pleasant to work with, and they bring the level of performance up for the entire team. Who knows why some employees are that way? That's really not the point. Even if we knew, it still would be tough to find and recruit them. The point is to make sure that employees find enough value in working with the organization to want to stay.

Let's be clear, though. In no sense do we need to bow down and put ourselves at the mercy of any employee who makes excessive and unreasonable demands, no matter how good that employee is. We are talking about good or great employees who simply know that they do a fine job and that they are very marketable. They know, quite justifiably, that great employees are worth something and are always in demand.

The Idea in Action

Andy managed a fast-food restaurant. He found the high turnover of employees disturbing. He was dismayed with the time and energy costs in the hiring process. Despite the large number of part-time employees, Andy was soon able to identify the poor and good performers. Having identified the good employees, he was upset to find them leaving so often. He knew that he could not stop the trend totally.

However, he decided to do what he could to improve the situation. He conducted fair and honest performance reviews so that he could offer a real pay differential to those who performed well. He promoted two of his best people to full-time assistant managers. With this action, Andy had two fine employees who would probably stay longer.

He took special care to thank, acknowledge, and work with them—especially the really good workers. They made a very valuable contribution to his operation and he knew it. He made sure they knew it also.

For Reflection

What do you do to retain top talent?

Thinking back over last year, why did some good employees leave?

How do you allocate your attention between poorly performing employees and top performers?

14

EDUCATE YOUR WORKERS ON THE ECONOMICS OF BUSINESS

Share information. Educate your workers—help them understand what you face. That makes them partners, not adversaries.

In More Depth

Most people are woefully uneducated and unaware of economics, particularly the economics of operating an organization. They have very little understanding of the costs of operations.

When people do not understand organizational economics, they operate under the false belief that there should always be more money available: for them, for everything they want, for any project which sounds interesting, or for more people to be hired. When this money is not available or forthcoming, people will become angry at management, their peers, and the organization.

People in for-profit businesses especially need to understand organizational economics. For whatever reason, many people do not realize that without profits, there will be no jobs or benefits. There will be no business, period.

By educating people on the basic economics of running an organization, you give them a greater appreciation of your job as manager. You are making them partners, rather than adversaries.

The Idea in Action

Angela owned a six-store chain of beauty parlors. She was facing some tough decisions. The salons were producing a reasonable return on her investment, though barely more than she would make if she were to sell them and invest that money. On the other hand, she liked having her own business.

Angela constantly had to deal with employees who felt that they were underpaid, that she should spend more on decor, that she should hire extra people, and so on. It seemed that they simply didn't understand the basic economics of operating a business.

She wanted to be fair with them. At the same time, she had to make enough profit to pay her business loan and to earn a fair profit.

She conducted a training session on the economics of running a business: the cost of borrowing, the need to produce a profit in order to stay in business and provide jobs, and more. To her surprise, the employees enjoyed learning about this stuff. They were amazed at how much the rent was, how much utilities cost, and how much Angela was spending on benefits.

Now, the employees still want raises. The difference is that they know in order to have raises the revenues must go up, so they help sell more and do what it takes to make the business profitable.

For Reflection

How would you characterize your employees' knowledge of organizational economics? Economics in general?

How about your knowledge of economics?

What would it take for you to put together a short, simple seminar on the economics and financial operations of an organization?

15

PERFORMANCE REVIEWS MUST MEAN SOMETHING

Give real, helpful, and constructive feedback during performance reviews. Otherwise, they are a waste of time. Tell people specifically what they do well and what they need to do to improve. Then help them set the vision of how they should perform for the next review.

In More Depth

Conducting performance reviews can strike fear in the hearts of most managers. Actually, it is a very important and powerful management tool. The key is to make it a valuable experience for you and the employee. This means that you need to give meaningful feedback—feedback which is honest and constructive.

Too often, performance reviews are perfunctory exercises which accomplish little except to raise stress levels. When the review is simply an exercise which glosses over real issues, when it gives lukewarm acknowledgment for a job well done or for a job poorly done (so as to avoid a potential unpleasant conversation), or when it is simply a bunch of boxes checked "meets standards"—you are wasting your time.

When you establish achievement levels, you will find that your performance reviews become very powerful motivating tools. Your employees will benefit and you will certainly find management a great deal easier.

The Idea in Action

Rustam managed a project for the federal government. He had never taken a management course, so he learned primarily from watching other managers within the system. When it came time to conduct performance reviews, he simply carried out the same exercise which had been done for him: checking the boxes, trying to get as many checks in the "meets criteria" box as possible.

As a result of a GAO audit, all managers attended a series of workshops. One of these was "How to Conduct Performance Reviews." The facilitator explained that the performance review could be a very important exercise to reduce unwanted employee behavior as well as motivate positive behavior. Rustam thought, "Sure, and it is a hassle." After some intense discussion, however, he decided that he really had nothing to lose.

He focused on his assistant managers. First, he established exactly what it was that he expected. To his surprise, he discovered that he didn't really know.

After he established clear expectations, the managers met. All said that they appreciated the specific direction. They felt like they now could move toward these goals. He gave his employees honest and forthright feedback. They talked until both parties were clear about their performance.

For Reflection

How helpful and constructive would your employees say your performance reviews are?

How much time do you spend writing and giving performance reviews?
What could you do to improve your performance review process?

16
THERE IS NO SUCH THING AS AN ORGANIZATION—
THERE ARE ONLY PEOPLE

Without people, you have no organization. Yes, you may have buildings, machinery, and bank accounts, but see how far that gets you without people. People are your most valuable asset. Treat them accordingly.

In More Depth

We too often speak of the business, the institute, the association, the company, the organization. We forget that those are only shells of something. Without people in those businesses and organizations, there is not much of anything left. There may be some legal papers, a building, machinery, and perhaps some money—but there really isn't an organization.

Buildings don't produce anything. Machinery does not serve a client or customer. Money does not do anything until it is used or invested. When we see through this illusion, we quickly realize that all we really have is our people. How easy it is to forget that. As managers, we need to constantly remind ourselves that our organization exists only because of the employees.

When we come to realize that all we really have is people, we begin to treat them with greater respect. We tend to put our attention and effort on them. Doing so produces results!

People are your most valuable asset. You have nothing without them. Act accordingly and you will be well rewarded.

The Idea in Action

Alex was general manager of a packaging plant. He held a militaristic view of management: "factors of production." He actually wished that he could get rid of all the people and just have robots and machinery, with automated systems and financial tracking.

Oddly enough, some of his employees liked him. The union was even cooperative. When Alex wanted to install some robots, he was amazed that the union agreed. (He actually thought he had tricked them.) When the robots were installed, one problem followed another. In fact, Alex had to hire more union members to operate and maintain the system. (The union members just smiled.)

Then Alex wanted to get rid of the accounting people and "contract out the services." When the contract was let, Alex found that he had to deal with a representative from the contracting company. The contractor did not understand the plant's accounting system well and there were reporting errors, delays, and misunderstandings. Alex knew he had made a mistake, but hated to admit it.

After two tries at having an organization without people, he had learned his lesson. It was a hard lesson for him, but an important one.

For Reflection

What would you have if your "organization" had no people?

Do you treat your employees as the most valuable "factor of production" or as the least important?

What could you do that would use the "leverage point" of people within your organization?

17

DEVELOP PEOPLE BY GIVING THEM A CHANCE

The old word is delegation. Give your employees a chance. Give them clear direction with clear tasks to accomplish along with the responsibility to achieve them. Then give them the time, space, resources, and authority to succeed.

In More Depth

You need to develop your people. You do so by giving them a chance. You will want to give clear directions, help people understand your expectations, and provide them with the ability to get the job done. Then let them go and achieve those objectives.

One might think of people development as delegation. It is, but it goes beyond that. In the purest sense, delegation is having people do work for you which you cannot or should not be doing yourself, but work for which you are responsible. In developing employees, you focus on delegating the task *and* giving people the chance to grow in the process. As a result, you not only get the work done but also have more competent people to assist you in achieving the organization's goals.

In order to develop your employees by giving them a chance, you must give them the responsibility to achieve the assigned task or objective. Then you must provide them with the wherewithal to be able to do it. That means you must give them the time, space, resources, and authority to succeed.

The Idea in Action

Jolene was district manager for a chain of candy stores. She was being considered for a promotion.

The vice president met with each candidate, asking several questions. Among them: "What would the company do if something happened to you? Are there?> people who could fill your shoes?" Two candidates answered, "No, I work so hard and carry so much responsibility that it would be difficult to replace me." They were quickly removed from the list.

That left Jolene and one other. The other answered, "I do have some good people who could fill my place. I've hired well and have several people with talent." The VP thought this answer was an improvement, but didn't get at the heart of what he was looking for. He knew that it was critical to develop people.

When Jolene's turn came, she answered, "Sam could; so could Sally; in fact, there are a number of managers who could take my place." The VP quizzed, "How can you be sure?" She answered, "Because I develop people by giving them a chance—a chance to succeed. I work with them on setting clear objectives. I then make sure they have the resources to accomplish the task at hand. They usually succeed."

The VP was impressed.

For Reflection

How do you develop your people?

How do you give them a chance?

What would your employees say about your "developing them by giving them a chance"?

18

SURROUND YOURSELF WITH THE BEST PEOPLE POSSIBLE

Search for, recruit, and hire the best people possible. By doing so, you simply stack the deck in favor of your organization.

In More Depth

Your goal is to achieve your organizational objectives. The easiest way to do so is to have people who can help you. Many times, managers fall into the trap of seeing people as "units of production." There is a better way. See them as the magic in an organization. See them as the fire which can ignite an explosion of productivity. The truth remains that you really need to have the best people possible in order to make the magic happen.

You may have to spend more time than you'd like finding the best employees to recruit and hire. It is difficult work, but it is well worth the effort. Those extra hours pay huge dividends.

Managers succeed through their people. No manager can do it alone. To accomplish big results, you need top-drawer people—people who perform well under any circumstance. There is no perfect way to know who these people are, but you can make some high-probability bets by looking at their history. Winners win—again and again. Once you have identified the winners, make it a top priority to surround yourself with such talent.

The Idea in Action

Sharon had purchased a franchise "copy shop." The most formidable challenge facing her was the competition. There were shops everywhere. However, she had a plan. She would get the best salespeople possible.

Sharon spent 2 weeks personally calling on organizations and asking them about their copying needs. (She was after more than their copying business.) When she was told, "We're getting great service now," she found what she was looking for. She asked for the name of the sales and service representative. After several weeks, about 10 names kept coming up in her conversations. Sharon reasoned that these were probably the 10 best salespeople in town.

Sharon made a point of getting to know these salespeople. She recruited them. She was ultimately able to hire several.

With the top salespeople in town, Sharon's business exploded. They were top producers. When Sharon hired other staff, she took similar care to hire the best people. With so many top performers, the teamwork and productivity was electric. Everyone was inspired. It was a place which set high standards and met those high standards by having the very best people possible.

For Reflection

If you were ranking your employees, how many would you say are "the best people possible"?

How do you recruit, hire, and retain the best people possible?

What could you do now to build a team of the best people possible?

Working with People

19

CREATE RELATIONSHIPS

You build trust when you build relationships. Trust improves morale and productivity with your team and it builds loyalty from your customers.

In More Depth

To be successful as a manager, you must build relationships. You must certainly create relationships with customers, but just as important is the relationship you create with your team of employees and colleagues.

The payoff to creating true relationships is obvious: *trust.* If you're my boss and we trust each other, I am more likely to follow your leadership and you are more likely to allow me some freedom as long as I get the job done. We don't spend a lot of time and energy "watching our backs." We take intelligent risks because we are confident of the other's response. We pull harder for each other, back each other up, and go the extra mile.

It seems so simple. Why don't more managers do this? Because building relationships takes work, and it can be frightening to be "real." You do not have to develop a personal friendship. You do have to develop a good working relationship. That is, if you want great results.

The Idea in Action

Trebor was a warehouse supervisor. While personable, he did not particularly like to become "chummy" with employees.

One time the company did an employee survey. Employees in Trebor's area felt that he did not "care about them as people." Rather, they said that he preferred to issue orders.

The vice president told Trebor that he needed to build relationships with his employees. Trebor was both a little angry and a lot worried about how to go about building these relationships. "After all," he thought, "I do my work. I don't mistreat anyone. I just have a job to do and I expect others to do theirs."

He tried being a little more friendly, but it was hard. Trebor talked with the VP and told him of his concern. "Why didn't you speak up sooner?" was the VP's big-brotherly response. "I used to feel that way too, until I realized that I was building relationships, not to make friends, but to be approachable—human—and understanding. Just take an interest in people and what they are thinking and saying. Give them feedback. Show appreciation and tell them when they do well."

Trebor was relieved. Now that he understood, he felt that he could learn to build relationships and that it could actually be fun.

For Reflection

How do you build relationships with your employees?
How do you build relationships with your colleagues and bosses?
How well do you know your employees?

20
DON'T KILL THE MESSENGER

You must have accurate information. Your career and your organization depend upon that. People must not fear bringing you bad news or fear telling you things you don't like to hear. If you kill the messenger, you end up hearing only half-truths. Thank the messenger.

In More Depth

We've all heard, "Don't kill the messenger," and many of us have actually said that to someone to whom we were delivering bad or unpleasant news.

The reasoning is simple: If you kill the messenger, you will stop getting messages (at least accurate and important ones). Managers and leaders depend on information, and it is vital that information be true, valid, and unvarnished. When you start relying on filtered, modified, and sugar-coated information, you lose your strength in having that information.

People kill messengers because they confuse the messenger and the message. It is the message that you want. You can't be everyone and talk to everyone. So your staff and your colleagues are your ears and eyes, and thus can be your messengers.

Actions must now speak louder than words. You may have to prompt people to tell you a little bad news. When they do gingerly tell you, respond with openness and appreciation for *their* openness and honesty. They will follow your lead.

The Idea in Action

Yeoman was the owner of an import/export company. He was used to being right. So when employees and customers came to him complaining that something was wrong or that something bad had happened, he would explode. "How could this happen?" he would bellow. "Who says so?" he would interrogate. "Why did you let that happen?"

Not surprisingly, his employees avoided him. As a result, Yeoman was "out of the loop" on developing problems, potentially negative situations, and trends which his employees saw. Yeoman would hear of problems only when they were big and no longer could be avoided. He didn't get a chance to deal with them when they were minor and could have been easily handled.

One night as he was taking his Mylanta for his ulcer, he realized that he had been killing the messengers. He was quite dismayed when he finally understood that he was the cause of the problem and that it was only natural for people to withhold information from him.

He set about the very next day to remedy the situation. Being a wise man, he knew that he had to demonstrate his commitment to this new way of being, so he was absolutely determined to respond with openness and appreciation when some unpleasant news was brought to him.

For Reflection

Can you remember the last time you killed the messenger?

How do your employees communicate bad news to you?

How did it feel when you were "killed" after delivering a bad-news message? What was the result?

21
COMPASSION IS A BUSINESS ASSET

Compassion comes with the confidence to be gentle, while remaining strong. It is understanding, caring, and sometimes forgiving—potent and powerful human motivators. Having and showing compassion will build loyalty.

In More Depth

Compassion could be described as having an emotional understanding of another person's troubling situation. Granted, that situation technically isn't your problem. On the other hand, it is directly your problem. You manage people, not machines. People have emotions, experience problems, and make mistakes. Compassion is the capacity to understand on more than a mental level that another person (your employee, colleague, or boss) is human, *just like you.*

Having compassion in these situations goes further than just understanding. How much further depends on the circumstance, but you must let the other person know that you care and understand. You can do something to demonstrate your understanding: take the employee out for coffee to talk about the problem, send a note or some small acknowledgment (like flowers, if there has been a death in the family).

When we show compassion, understanding, caring, and forgiving, we ignite powerful human motivators. People notice. They respond. Compassion builds loyalty and motivation.

The Idea in Action

Gina ran a large warehouse. She was a task-oriented manager. "Just get the work done" was her motto.

One day a clerk messed up in a big way. Gina became furious. She suspended him for 2 days. She was having trouble sleeping and the man's eyes kept appearing. "Something was sad about those eyes," she thought. She was so disturbed that she called him at home the next morning.

She asked him to come in. The clerk feared that he was going to be fired. "Please sit down," Gina said softly. "I want to talk about my behavior yesterday. I was wrong. I didn't take time to find out your side of the story or what may have caused it. Would you please tell me?"

The clerk was shocked and skeptical, but figured he had nothing to lose. "I was wrong in the way I did the order, but I was so upset I couldn't think. My wife just asked for a divorce." Gina felt a stab of pain go through her.

She gently asked, "Do you need a little time off to help you get it worked out?" Her compassion amazed him, especially given Gina's tough reputation.

Gina began to show compassion over time. She did not lower her standards; she raised her humanity.

For Reflection

What is your favorite story about a time when you showed compassion?

Are you able to show compassion when the situation warrants it?

What would the payoff be to you and your organization if you were known as an effective and compassionate boss?

22

SEE THE POSITIVE SIDE OF CONFLICT

Conflict is a chance to put things on track. Conflict can bring clarity. You can use its energy to move everyone forward.

In More Depth

While not always pleasant or comfortable, conflict has its positive side. Conflict is a cry to get things back on track — to have things work again—things which are in a broken state. The appearance of conflict can be viewed positively. Consider that the parties must want to make things work; otherwise, they wouldn't bother with the conflict. The key is to realize that conflict in itself is not a threat and that the way people engage in conflict can either be an opportunity or an additional problem.

Conflict helps people understand other people's point of view, as well as their own. When people understand where others stand and think, there is a possibility of working with them in a much more authentic way. Time and energy are not diminished with the underlying conflict or the attempt to avoid it.

Conflict is not comfortable, nor does it mean that everybody will be happy or get everything they want. Facing conflict gives it a chance to be resolved, whereas avoidance makes sure it stays around. It offers a possibility for getting back on track. When conflicts are resolved, morale always improves.

The Idea in Action

Poshi was manager of the computer department. He was kind and gentle. He hated conflict and didn't want to hurt anyone's feelings.

He was hearing complaints between members of the team. He phoned the head of human resources and asked for guidance. She said, "Poshi, you're a nice man and you were brought up to avoid conflict. That simply isn't working in this case. Avoiding the conflicts is not making them go away; it is exacerbating them."

He took her advice and started the next day. He called in the two people who had the biggest conflict. He started, "I'm uncomfortable with this situation, but we have a problem here. We need to address it and discuss it. We need to communicate responsibly and we need to be sensitive to one another as colleagues and human beings. We need to tell the truth, without attacking, and we need to know what we are headed for: In this case, we are headed for a resolution which will allow us to work together better."

The employees were shocked, but ultimately pleased, that Poshi had not shrunk from the conflict. In fact, he embraced it and found a positive side to it.

For Reflection

How do you feel about engaging in conflict?
What is your favorite story about how conflict had a positive outcome?
What conflicts are boiling underneath the surface in your organization?

23

DIFFERENT SITUATIONS DEMAND DIFFERENT LEADERSHIP STYLES

Vary your style depending on the situation. No two situations or people are the same. Step back and see what will work best to accomplish your goal.

In More Depth

Leadership may require you to be very direct, take charge and lead the troops. At other times you may need to "sell" more than "tell." Then there are the times when you must be very sensitive and respond to the tender human aspects of your organization and at still other times you may need to be very detail and process oriented. The goal and the situation will set the foundation for the style of leadership to employ. Obviously, this requires an accurate assessment of the situation and a clear understanding of your goal.

You have a particular leadership style. This style will be your dominant one. However, to be successful you will need to flex your "style muscles" and shift to what is needed at any particular time.

The Idea in Action

Bette was transferred to a department which had established a reputation for being slow and inefficient. She was a powerful and dominant leader. She immediately established a strong presence. She "told it like it was" and demanded that her people move forward with projects.

She shook the place up. She fired a few people, a few others left "for personal reasons," and the rest settled in for the duration.

Most people rallied to the cause. Although they complained a little, they did notice that their work improved and that they were getting some recognition from other departments. Over the next 6 months, they developed pride in their work and eventually came to like Bette as a leader.

When the major changes had been integrated, Bette realized that while the level of tension in the organization was appropriate for a "high change" atmosphere, it was not appropriate for a team that needed to focus on stabilizing. Her dominant and demanding style needed to change. The organization needed more of a coaching and supportive style with someone who would guide people in focusing on quality.

Bette adjusted her style and focused on coaching people in the quality control efforts, and offering lots of support when improvements were made. She had successfully adapted her style to the needs of the organization.

For Reflection

What leadership style does your organization need today?
How would you characterize your predominate leadership style?
How many leadership styles do you have in your arsenal?

24

SET CLEAR EXPECTATIONS

Tell your employees what you expect. Be specific. By doing so, you set up the "game" in such a way that people know how to "win."

In More Depth

All of us want to be winners. In order to win, we must know the rules of the game. We must know what it takes to win; otherwise, we're just running around on the playing field without knowing what to do or where to go. People must know what it takes to be successful in order for them to achieve success.

This is a little different from setting goals. Developing and/or sharing goals with your team is like telling people the object of the game and where the finish line is. By setting clear expectations, on the other hand, you are giving each player a game plan which fits into the whole.

When you set and communicate these expectations, be very specific. Tell people exactly what you want and expect. Describe it for them. Perhaps even show them. Ask them if they understand. When people know what is expected of them, that's usually what they will do. People cannot possibly meet your expectations unless they know what they are.

The Idea in Action

Barbara became assistant manager of a tourist shop. Most of the employees were college students off for the summer. They wanted to "hang out" as much as they wanted to work. Barbara wanted to be liked and was very tolerant at first.

A lot of work wasn't getting done. Barbara knew instinctively that her leadership was inadequate and vowed to improve. Since she had never taken any formal management courses, she relied on her child-rearing experience. She remembered: When she was specific and set clear expectations, that is what her children did. In the absence of clear expectations, they did it their own way.

Barbara tried this. Calling a meeting, she said, "Beginning today, I need to let you know what I expect from each of you. Tom, you're to clean the book area. Take each shelf down and rearrange it to its proper height. Jane, you're to arrange the maps in order, starting with the one closest to this location." She continued with specific and clear expectations for each employee.

To her delight, they all did wonderfully. From that point on, Barbara set and communicated clear expectations for each employee. She would thank and praise them when they met those expectations. Everyone pulled together and the store ran marvelously.

For Reflection

Do you set clear expectations for each of your employees?
How do you communicate expectations?
Why do you think that setting clear expectations works so well?

25
DON'T VIOLATE CONFIDENCES

Keep your promises about confidences and confidential matters. Be clear with people if there is something which you cannot keep confidential. Consider granting "anonymity" rather than promising to keep something secret—it's less constraining and still gains you respect.

In More Depth

The importance of maintaining confidences cannot be overstated. This rule is about interpersonal matters, not confidential information such as personnel records and legal matters which require legal confidentiality.

You must develop trust between you and your employees. One of the most visible ways to develop trust is to honor confidentiality. When trusted, you are able to have more open dialogues. You are given more information. You hear about issues earlier. You can discuss and wrestle with the "real" issues rather than the surface ones.

Whether it is personal information or organizational information, honor its confidential nature. When the information is organizationally important, find some way to deal with it without violating the confidentiality. Consider working with anonymity instead. Guard the personal trust your employees place in you.

The Idea in Action

Jairo started an import/export business. One day, an assistant manager told him, "You know Julie? Well she is having troubles at home. She told me confidentially about it last week. Also, David told me about what the guys are saying on the loading dock. He asked me to keep it confidential, but I will tell you...."

Jairo could stand no more. He said, "Why are you telling me this? Didn't you agree to keep it confidential? Can't anyone trust your word? How many other people did you tell after you had given someone your bond of trust? When you tell someone that something is confidential, then keep it that way."

"If it affects this organization, then do something about it while maintaining the confidentiality. As for the personal stuff people told you, how dare you violate their trust? How would you feel if you told me something and asked me to keep it confidential—only to later find out that I told people? You'd never trust me again. As the leader of this organization, I need your trust. I have to earn it—not violate it."

Jairo realized that he had flown off the handle, so he softened a bit. "I understand the difficulty with confidentiality, especially with organizational issues. I almost never grant confidentiality. I just tell people that I will keep their disclosure anonymous. I build trust with them and they then develop trust in me."

For Reflection

How does it feel to have a confidence violated?

How do you establish open communication with your employees? Confidentiality? Anonymity? Discretion? Trust?

What would you tell one of your assistants about violating confidences?

Increasing
Productivity

26

DECIDE WHAT REALLY MAKES A CONTRIBUTION

Some decisions and actions are more important than others. Some get you much closer to your goals, others only inch you forward. Decide what is important. Spend your time and energy there.

In More Depth

As a manager you have too much to do. Most managers are pulled from one thing to the next in rapid-fire succession. Much of what managers do produces little value. We don't like to hear that, but down deep we know it is true. The key to being a successful manager is to decide what really makes a contribution to the organization and then do it.

Some tasks are simply more important than others. Some are more important at one time than at another. Some are nice, but don't make much difference. Some tasks we do simply because we like to do them regardless of their importance. Still others are downright unimportant and a waste of our managerial time.

Your time is valuable. For you to be the most effective that you can be as a manager, you must use your time wisely. That means doing only those tasks which make a real contribution. You will find yourself light-years ahead of those who waste time on trivial matters.

The Idea in Action

As district director of an insurance company, Arthur was in charge of the entire sales and marketing effort, as well as operational and administrative management for the district. He felt overwhelmed.

He asked his regional manager, "What do you think is wrong?" She offered, "You have to decide what will make a real contribution to your district and then do it. This goes beyond prioritizing. When you prioritize, you must put things in order: first, second, and third. You need to take a more substantial approach. Decide on the top 10 tasks that would make a real difference in the way things operate. Find some way to systematize or delegate the rest."

Arthur made a list of all the different duties and tasks he performed. Alongside he made four columns:

- Nice to do, but doesn't really add much
- Important, but doesn't require my attention
- Important and requires my attention
- Vital to growth and success of this district

He then made the commitment to himself to act on the most important. The payoff was enormous. He accomplished more, had more time, and felt more relaxed.

For Reflection

What percentage of your activities make a real contribution to your organization?

How do you decide whether a task makes a valuable contribution?

What are the five most important activities you must do for the success of your organization?

27

DESTROY BARRIERS AND ROADBLOCKS

People want to do their jobs, but are often blocked. Barriers and roadblocks keep them from getting the work done. If you just removed the barriers, you'd improve productivity dramatically. Find out what stops work from being done.

In More Depth

Barriers and roadblocks in an organization can kill productivity. Chop them down! Granted, management must have controls and policies, but almost everyone would agree that some policies and controls block effective work. The problem even grows because we often implement new policies, procedures, and controls *without removing the old ones.* So, we add layer upon layer of bureaucracy.

What is the easiest way to find the barriers or roadblocks? Ask! Ask employees what hinders them from doing a superb job. Then be ready for the answers. If a particular roadblock is legitimate and there is no compelling reason to keep the barrier there, destroy it. If there is a compelling reason to keep it, explain why it is important. Frequently, understanding a perceived barrier can diminish or eliminate the problem.

When people are not frustrated by barriers to getting their job done, productivity increases; so does morale. People are happier when they have fewer hassles.

The Idea in Action

Jackie was municipal department manager for a city. Her department was responsible for design and zoning compliance inspections.

The public thought her department was lazy and extremely bureaucratic. She was also aware that her staff members were very frustrated by what they perceived as difficulties in getting their job done. All in all, it was a very difficult situation.

She decided to attack the problems head-on. She knew that there were good reasons why some regulations were in place and why laws and safeguards were instituted. She also suspected that there were a lot of outdated procedures which could be improved; policies which needed review; and absolute foolishness which could be eliminated.

She asked every employee to list "the things that stop you from doing your work in the most efficient, effective, and enjoyable manner possible." (She took a risk when they included *enjoyable*, but figured, "What the heck. Why not go for broke?")

After Jackie and her team made the changes, the employees and public saw that she was serious. She was flooded with more suggestions and even some praise.

For Reflection

What is one barrier that stops you from doing your job in the best way possible?

Could you find 10 ways to destroy unproductive barriers in your organization?

How have you benefited from not removing roadblocks and barriers in your organization? (Sometimes we perceive a benefit from not solving a problem, and thus we perpetuate it.)

28

FOCUS ON PERFORMANCE, NOT PERSONALITY

Some personalities drive managers crazy. Performance counts; personalities don't. You don't need to like people in order for them to produce great results.

In More Depth

It's performance that counts. This is a primary rule. It is also one of the most frustrating. It can be very difficult to separate someone's personality from his or her performance, especially when that person has a "challenging" disposition.

A typical reaction is to ignore or try to get rid of the person. It is the wise and strong manager who realizes that people's actions are far more important than their style.

Learn to look for performance. See what the person does—beyond any difficulties with personality. Give it your best shot. If that person is doing a fine job, just let the employee continue the work. Obviously, if the employee is bothering others, you may have to do something about that.

Many organizations are filled with people who have great personalities but don't do much. Remember, it is difficult to find people who can get the job done. Personality is not the key to doing a great job.

The Idea in Action

Claudio was general manager for a wholesale bakery. When he asked people about morale, he was surprised to find that many of them didn't think that it was particularly low. He thought to himself, "How could morale not be low with Tom, Annamarie, JR, and Shannah around? They are the most difficult people in the world and they are always driving me crazy." He was projecting his own biases based on their personalities.

Claudio's younger brother, Vincent, came to visit him. Claudio told him of his frustration. "What should I do?" he asked. "What do you *need* to do?" Vincent replied. "I don't know, that's why I asked you," responded Claudio, feeling a little bit annoyed. His brother continued, "What I mean is this: You may not need to do anything except learn to accept and deal with people's personalities. Big brother, here are the real questions you should be asking: Do these people perform? Do they help you reach your goals? If they do, and if they are not damaging other people or your organization, you may not really have a problem."

Claudio considered Vincent's comment and had to admit that each of his headaches actually did do the job well. When he was willing to deal with their idiosyncrasies, things did seem to go OK—even if he didn't like having to bend to their quirkiness.

For Reflection

How would you describe the personalities of the three people who most annoy you at work?

Can you separate their performance from their personality?

What types of personalities trap you into negative reactions? Do they remind you of anyone in your early life?

29

HAVE A DESTINATION

Know where you are going. Design and follow a plan to get there. You'll get there faster, with less likelihood of being sidetracked.

In More Depth

You need to know where you are going. You must have a destination. You must decide where you want to arrive. Otherwise, you spend all your time just "driving around." When you have a destination, you can look at a map (your plan) and proceed toward your target.

Choose where you want to go. Set your targets. Establish goals and objectives. Once you establish goals, objectives, or targets, create a plan (a map) to get there. Then marshal all your resources to achieve your plan. You and your team are all heading in the same direction, toward the same destination. Use your time and energy to move toward the goal rather than having people waste their efforts going in alternate directions.

As with any trip, you will need to make midcourse adjustments. Imagine driving a car down the road. When you have the destination in mind, you can see which adjustments to make, which turns to take, and which paths to avoid. Knowing the destination allows you to drive there quicker, with much less likelihood of getting lost.

The Idea in Action

Steven was elected president of a community development organization. In recent years, the nonprofit had become more of a social organization. It had strayed from its purpose, and many felt that it was losing its direction.

Steven engaged the staff in a "needs assessment" to gauge people's thoughts about what the organization should be doing and where it should be going. To Steven's great disappointment, no clear consensus emerged.

He gathered the board of advisers together for a planning session. He began by locking the door behind him and saying, "We are not leaving here until we have a destination for this organization. We need to decide where we want to go and what we want to become. We need to decide how it is to work. We need to decide the best route to take. And we need to enjoy our journey."

Someone from the group yelled out, "Thank God! We're finally going to get somewhere!" They came to some clear conclusions which nearly everyone endorsed. Then they mapped out a strategy. All the advisers were tired when they left that evening, but they had a sense of purpose and achievement. They also were committed to reaching the goals.

For Reflection

Articulate the destination of your organization.
Would all your employees describe the same destination?
How will you celebrate when you get there?

30

SO YOU'RE DOING THINGS RIGHT: ARE YOU DOING THE RIGHT THINGS?

You're busy, but are you doing the right things? The right things move your organization forward, solve problems, and seize opportunities. What is really important?

In More Depth

You have two important functions as a manager: to do things right and to do the right things. The function with the greater impact on your organization is to do the right things. While that may appear obvious, it is amazing how many managers spend time doing the wrong things *right*.

Sometimes—no, actually most of the time—we must perform tasks which aren't very dramatic or interesting. Yet they move our organization closer to its goals. We are still "doing the right things," even though our contribution isn't dramatic. The problem is in those tasks and functions which really don't make a positive contribution. It's time to stop doing those—and the quicker we stop, the better. Every manager has only so much time and energy. Our responsibility is to use our time and energy on things that matter, on things that will make a contribution to the company.

The shift in focus can make a remarkable difference in your success. It is the very distinction between an outstanding manager or leader and a merely competent one.

The Idea in Action

Jeanne was sales manager for an office products company. She noticed that sales growth was slowing and team morale was slipping—while problems with existing customers were on the rise.

She was hiring-firing-motivating-supporting-teaching-training her staff, completing paperwork, dealing with customer complaints, and attending professional meetings—all the while trying to maintain a meaningful home life.

One night she threw up her hands and said, "I've about had it! I can't possibly do everything on my list. What am I going to do?"

She called her uncle. "So what do I do, Uncle Leroy?"

He replied: "Your problem, Jeanne, is that you are so focused on doing everything right that you have forgotten to ask yourself if you are doing the right things. You can do only so much. You must realize that some activities just aren't the right things for you to be doing."

The next day she began to examine what activities should command her attention. She eliminated some, reorganized others, delegated appropriate ones, and added a few activities which she had been ignoring but which made her time much more valuable.

For Reflection

How do you know if you are doing the right things?

What percentage of your to-do list is in the "doing the right things" category?

What three activities are you currently doing which don't make much of a contribution to your organization?

Understanding and Motivating the Team

31
RAISE THE FUN QUOTIENT

Fun adds flavor to a sometimes dull routine. Fun inspires and it energizes. Fun also builds relationship and morale. It pays to have fun!

In More Depth

It may seem a bit odd to include *fun* as a topic in a management book, but it is an important aspect to consider in your organization's operation.

This magic ingredient, fun, works on a simple psychological principle: If you enjoy what you're doing and if you like and enjoy the people around you, you tend to have more interest in your routine and more energy for being involved. By being more involved and more energized, you contribute more to the group. When you contribute more to the group, whose members are also having fun and enjoying themselves, it contributes more to you. Fun builds on itself. It is frequently self-sustaining. It's easy and costs little, if anything, to engender.

One of the secrets of a good organizational consultant is to notice if the people are having any fun. If they are, it's a clue that productivity and morale are probably higher than at most businesses.

The Idea in Action

Edgar is the executive director of a local charity. He has a tough job managing the operations and finances, and also motivating his team.

He used to enjoy his job a lot, but lately it had become dull and frustrating.

He noticed that volunteers were opting not to continue their service. Also, four full-timers had left. He was surprised, since most of the staffers tended to stay in their jobs for long periods. He talked with the people who had left and asked why.

They told him that they still believed in and cared about the clients, that they were proud of the organization, and that they respected Edgar as a manager. It's just that "the work wasn't fun anymore."

Edgar took their message to heart and also reviewed how he felt at his job. He asked himself: "Am I having fun here?" It was clear to him that he wasn't having as much fun as before either. "Time to do something!" he thought.

He quickly assembled a *fun team* consisting of three workers plus himself. They brainstormed about ways to infuse some excitement and joy back into the workplace. The team members set a goal of instigating one fun activity each week. They knew that fun was important. The next year more volunteers joined; turnover slowed to its former pace; and Edgar had more fun.

For Reflection

How does your organization promote fun?
What are two ways you could instigate some fun in the next week or so?
When was the last time you put fun and work together?

32
FEAR KILLS PRODUCTIVITY

People who are afraid spend their time, talent, and energy protecting themselves. You need their focus to be on the organization in order to move forward. Eliminate fear.

In More Depth

You have only to look to your own experience to find the truth in the saying "Fear kills." Remember a time when you were afraid: of saying something, of doing something, of taking a risk, of losing your job, of not getting a promotion, or anything else. During that time, were you at your best? Of course not. That is the problem. When fear overtakes your team, you are losing productivity, efficiency, and effectiveness.

When people are afraid, they spend time protecting themselves, their ideas, their territory, and the status quo. No one would argue against the concept that some prudence is healthy and that some impending actions are inherently frightening. The fear we are talking about here, however, is the kind that can be eliminated and, once eliminated, allows an organization to run better.

People have only so much time, talent, and creativity. Channel that energy in positive pursuits for the organization or lose that potential.

The Idea in Action

Wilma managed the district operations of a convenience store chain. She was "one tough manager," as her employees described her.

Her district's figures were only in the middle of the company's rankings. She asked her employees why. Their answers were pleasant but totally unenlightening. She was upset that they couldn't give her better answers.

Wilma asked a friend, "Jake, what's wrong?" He knew, but he hesitated to tell her. She caught his hesitation. "Just tell me," she implored. Jake began, "Actually, everyone is afraid of you. They think that if they disagree with you, you'll bite their heads off. They know that you get angry when you're told of a problem. So they hide things from you. They're also afraid of the company laying them off."

Wilma was shocked. "Jake, you know that I'm just a pussycat and there are no layoffs planned."

"Yes," he replied, "but they don't. You need to drive that fear out of your district."

Wilma tackled the problem. In a nutshell—she let her actions speak louder than her words. She went on a Drive Out the Fear campaign. It worked and now her district is a leader.

For Reflection

Are people who report to you afraid to speak out, disagree with you, or take informed risks?

Do employees visibly tense up when you arrive or have a difficult time making a coherent sentence when they speak to you?

What concrete steps can you take to drive out fear in your organization?

33

BE FAIR, LEST YOU FACE CONTEMPT AND OVERTHROW

Tyrants and dictators are eventually overthrown. Fairness keeps you from becoming a tyrant.

In More Depth

Some managers use their influence to grant favors to employees whom they like and to withhold rewards or punish those whom they dislike. If the boss gives rewards for outstanding performance, that is fine. If the punishment is for poor or inappropriate behavior, that is also fine. The problem arises when the manager does not deal fairly.

Some tyrannical managers believe that they can get by with doing thus. Nonsense. If you are unfair, your workers will sooner or later punish you. They can directly or indirectly go to your superiors. They can slow down their work. They can lay in wait until you stumble and then pile on you when you're down. They can engage in outright mutiny, doing things for which they will not be identified, but which will destroy your ability to operate successfully.

One of the best ways to be fair and to be known for fairness is to determine *what* is right, not *who* is right. When issues arise, look beyond personalities. Take the side of the right thing to do, rather than making it a personality issue.

The Idea in Action

Melissa was hired to replace the public information officer (PIO) of a northeastern city. The former PIO had been somewhat of a tyrant and had just resigned. Her staff had covertly taken actions which made it difficult for her to operate and made her life so miserable that she had little choice.

Melissa was younger and had less experience than most of her staff members. Yet she was fair and fair-minded. She demonstrated her commitment to fairness the very first day she assumed her position. After she had addressed her staff for the first time, one employee asked, "Will you stop the people over in duplicating services from delaying our orders?"

Melissa replied, "I don't know. I intend to be fair in all situations. I will have to learn more from both sides to see what is right in this situation. I always look for what is right, not who is right and not who can make the most noise."

Her reputation for fairness grew. It was not always the easy path. She would have loved to reward her close supporters and bully the people who gave her grief, but she stuck to being fair.

For Reflection

When was the last time you had to make a decision on the basis of fairness?

Do you treat favored employees the same as less favored employees?

If your employees were asked, "Are you a fair manager?" how would they respond?

34

DON'T PLAY GAMES WITH PEOPLE'S PAY

Fair compensation involves integrity, morality, and legality. Don't play games with people's pay. You'll lose—lose respect as well as lawsuits.

In More Depth

Nothing is more dear to an employee's heart—and to most managers' hearts—than that paycheck. Be fair. Rigorously live up to every written and oral agreement or promise you make. If you lose your integrity on this issue, there will be nothing you can do to regain an employee's loyalty.

Whenever managers play games with compensation, they risk losing respect. Worse, they are perceived as dishonest, immoral, mean, and interested only in themselves at the expense of their employees. When that perception develops, the employees' behavior will begin to match the manager's, and the employees will begin to look out for themselves at the expense of the organization.

The Idea in Action

Roger was the son of the founder of a metropolitan newspaper. There was a lot of pressure on him to be as successful as his father, Bill. Bill was also well known for being a tough SOB when it came to dealing with employees. Bill was semiretired and came into work for only a few hours every day, but he liked to meddle while he was there.

Bill told him, "Son, in order to be a success in this business, you have to make sure you keep everyone else's hand from going into your pocket. You have to watch their every move!" Bill would "sort of" promise something and never come through, making up an excuse later. There was talk of unionizing the plant because of his shenanigans, and a couple of lawsuits had been filed under fair compensation laws.

One day Roger heard about his father's latest game with an employee's pay. It seems that the company's top advertising salesman had achieved a bonus level much faster than Bill had thought possible so he had gone in and tried to recalculate the commissions.

Roger finally had enough. It was time for him to assert his leadership. He confronted his father and said, "Dad, you have been a very successful businessman. I am proud of you, but we have some problems here which we must correct. We can no longer play with people's pay. We are wrong on this issue." Roger and his father fought that day. As a result, each came to understand the other better.

Roger gained the respect of the employees by immediately reviewing and correcting any pay issues. He paid fairly and honorably, while still maintaining profitability.

For Reflection

What games have been played in your organization around the issue of people's pay?

How would you feel if someone played games with your compensation?

What direct as well as covert responses do you think employees engage in when managers play with their pay?

35
PEOPLE NEED ROOTS

People must have stability in their lives. They need to belong. They need to feel secure. They can deal with only so much change and chaos. Help give your people "roots."

In More Depth

As a manager, you are well advised to help people feel "rooted" in your organization. "Rooted" means that people feel secure—sensing that this place or this job is their home and they are not going to be attacked, abused, or thrown out.

People need stability in their lives. They can deal with change. They can adjust. They can even accept the inevitable. What people *cannot* do is live in that state of fear and apprehension forever. At some point, they must return to feeling "rooted."

Employees need to feel that they are part of the organization. Belonging is very important. It gives meaning and purpose to people's lives. They begin to help one another. They pull for the common good. A sense of belonging gives people the opportunity to focus on their work instead of their situation.

The Idea in Action

Andre was vice president of an investment firm. His informal title was Man With a Heart. Now don't conclude that he was a softie or that he couldn't be very tough. What earned him the nickname Man

With a Heart was his sensitivity to people and his understanding of their needs.

Andre had seen the effect of economic cycles on investment houses. In boom times, investment houses would hire like mad, only to announce mass layoffs when the inevitable economic cycle turned.

Andre knew that people needed roots. He also knew that he operated in a hopelessly chaotic business world. He balanced these two somewhat antithetical facts by being sensitive to the employees. For example, in good times he would hire only as many people as he absolutely needed, so that fewer would have to be laid off when the down times came. They loved him for that.

Andre did many other things to give employees a sense of belonging. He encouraged his managers and employees to get to know each other. He made sure that there was a place people could call their own, even if it was a little cubicle in the corner. They could decorate it and make it theirs.

Andre didn't see himself as being different from any other executive. He just knew it was his job to keep turnover low, productivity high, efficiency at a peak. Thus, he couldn't quite understand, but sincerely appreciated, the title that had been informally bestowed on him.

For Reflection

How do you give people roots within your organization?

What actions or behaviors have you observed on the part of people who do not feel that they have roots?

How would your performance change if you didn't feel secure, didn't feel like you belonged, and didn't feel like your job was stable?

36

ENCOURAGE INVOLVEMENT

Involvement increases commitment. Get your people involved. When appropriate, have them help make the decisions and do the planning. Involvement will make them much more invested in the outcome.

In More Depth

Get your people involved in planning, in providing input, and in making decisions. Involvement increases commitment. It's commitment that produces results. By getting people involved, you gain the benefit of having different perspectives to guide you in making top-quality plans and decisions.

When people are involved, they take more ownership of the decision process and the outcome. It's their plan and their egos which are on the line. That is a powerful motivator. Involvement gets the juices flowing.

Involving people means that you must give up some control and some time. Involvement builds morale and eases the burden of management. It enjoys the benefit of having the best minds working on problems and opportunities.

The Idea in Action

Derek was to head the planning and implementation of the 5-year sales plan. He worked on the plan day and night for over a month. He was so proud of his creation that he could hardly wait to unveil it to the troops.

The first stop was Kansas City. The salespeople sat there and listened attentively. He thought he had a winner on his hands. It was during the question-and-answer session that things started unraveling. People asked very pointed questions, with him being stumped on more than a few. It was fast becoming clear that he had made a major tactical error. He hadn't involved anyone in the planning process.

He could have continued to press his cause, but he knew that it was inherently flawed. He figured it was better to bite the bullet now and go back to the drawing board.

He changed his approach. He held planning meetings to develop the final draft. Derek encouraged involvement, which he got in abundance. He admitted that the redrawn plan was far better, having gone through this process, than was his original.

Derek was concerned that he had lost too much time by involving all the salespeople. To his surprise, the implementation phase of the plan went far faster because of it. Later, he involved the salespeople with the implementation phase. By involving people, Derek won. Time was not wasted, a better plan than ever was developed, and people were committed to making it work.

For Reflection

How do you involve your employees?

Does it bother you to have to spend the time that it takes to involve people? How do you discipline yourself to do it anyway?

What benefits do you see in involving people?

37

MAKE SURE THERE IS A PAYOFF FOR PEOPLE

There has to be value for everyone involved. When people feel like there is some payoff, there is more interest and motivation, and better results.

In More Depth

People get involved when there is a payoff. If there is no payoff, their hearts usually lie elsewhere. As a manager, then, you need to make sure that people see the payoff to whatever you have them doing.

Managers need to review what payoffs their employees get from their work and from the organization itself. There are salaries, bonuses, incentives, awards, promotions, recognition, public appreciation, names on a plaque, celebrations, sincere thank-yous, upgrades in work levels, and so on.

There must be value for everyone: the organization, the management, the employees, the stockholders, and the customers. When people realize the payoff, they become much more interested in the job and in the organization. There is more motivation and, thus, better results.

The Idea in Action

Donna was the general manager of a corporate farming operation. Because of her nontraditional role, she felt that she needed to demonstrate that she knew what she was doing. She would go out into the fields and stockyards with the workers. Most were very impressed by the end of her tour.

Donna had heard early in her career that it was impossible to motivate manual laborers. She knew better than that. "You just have to see things from their perspective," she'd say.

Donna made a special point of talking with her employees. She could "talk their talk" and she knew what payoffs they wanted. She instituted an incentive program for workers who exceeded the basic requirements of their jobs, with clarity about how they could achieve that goal.

Donna knew that camaraderie was a big payoff with the workers, so she held a big barbecue with music and dancing on one Friday night of each month. If the workers met certain objectives for the quarter, she would make a big deal of presenting awards at the hoedown. She always gave prizes and awards that meant something—fancy cowboy hats, silver belt buckles, and pairs of the best boots money could buy.

Donna had to fight with corporate headquarters in order to provide some of these payoffs. Many executives just couldn't see their value. Donna knew better. She made sure there were payoffs—and she got a big payoff in return by being recognized as one of the best managers in the entire operation.

For Reflection

What payoffs motivate your employees?

What payoffs could you highlight with your employees which you have not brought to light so far?

Would you be motivated if there were no payoff for your hard work?

Making Things Work

38
KEEP IT SIMPLE

Stick with the basics. The basics of management still work. Prepare, plan, think, listen, motivate, and appreciate employees; be responsible, work hard, make decisions, and execute.

In More Depth

Remember to keep it simple and stick with the basics. Sure you will want to explore new ideas, but the tried-and-true basics work. They aren't very glitzy or glamorous. What the basics do is produce results.

Many business leaders will admit privately that they have gone down the path of searching for sophisticated new approaches to operating their businesses. They will also admit that if they had just stayed with the basics and kept it simple, they would probably have been better off.

Management fads come and go—see if they have any value but keep it simple. A ship which changes direction with every shifting wind never gets to port. In the long run, keeping it simple and sticking with the basics works.

The Idea in Action

Charles was vice president of operations for a regional banking concern. He didn't have an MBA, but he would always listen to people's ideas and search for value in their ways of thinking. He didn't want to be left behind the times, so he went along with many of his colleagues' suggestions for changing the organization—its processes, the way it dealt with people, and its structure.

Charles noticed that with each *new* strategy, productivity initially went down. He dismissed this development, thinking, "Anything new will take some time to adjust." When productivity returned to earlier levels and morale improved, he noticed that there were no *dramatic* increases.

Charles began hearing from employees. They were asking, "Why don't we choose a strategy and stick with it?" Even though Charles had a plausible answer, his gut instinct told him that keeping it simple and sticking with basics would produce just as much without the disruption.

Charles shared his feelings with his colleagues. "Why don't we just try to keep it simple?" he asked. "We'll assess our organization, we'll map out some proven strategies. We'll commit ourselves to achieving our goals; communicate with our employees; offer true value to our customers; and adjust the plan as necessary. We'll reward excellence, get rid of incompetence, engage in dialogue, and work together.

The management team did just that. Everyone worked hard and kept it simple. People knew what to expect. They understood and got behind the plan.

For Reflection

What are three simple rules you have about making your organization work?

How would "keeping it simple" affect your management team, employees, and customers?

Why do you think some managers make things complex or jump to the management fad of the year?

39

SILENCE ISN'T GOLDEN

People change only when they get feedback—good or bad. To increase desirable behavior, give positive feedback. To reduce or eliminate undesirable behavior, tell people what's wrong and how to improve.

In More Depth

Everyone wants to be a winner. How do you, as a manager, set your people up and help them win? You give them feedback. You tell them what they are doing well, what they are doing badly, and what they need to do to get the job done.

People look to you for guidance. In the absence of feedback, people make up what they think you are thinking—or they make up what they want to believe. Feedback ends fantasy and gives clear direction.

Feedback is critical during performance reviews, but it may actually be more powerful when given informally. Don't wait for review time. Make it a habit to offer feedback regularly.

The Idea in Action

Adam was recruited and became director of the parks and recreation department. He began studying the department. He quickly learned that the efficiency, productivity, and morale of the department were miserable.

Adam knew that he could not just walk in and change everything, especially since the department was a civil service operation. He wondered what he could do to make the greatest difference.

He took a walk one evening with his girlfriend Stacey, a dog trainer. He told her of his concerns. Stacey simply asked, "Do people know what they are supposed to do?" Adam shrugged his shoulders. "I know people are different from dogs," Stacey continued, "but the way I get a dog to perform is by rewarding it when it does something right and punishing it when it does something wrong. The dog has to know what it is to do before it can do it." Adam knew that Stacey had stumbled onto the key: giving clear and honest feedback.

Adam made giving feedback a top priority. After meeting with his management team, he called a general meeting of all employees. He told them what the group was doing well and what it was doing poorly. He said, "From now on, I will tell each member of my management team what he or she is doing well and what needs to be improved. They will do the same with you."

Adam lived up to his commitment. His managers shaped up and became incredibly effective. The managers experienced even greater success with their employees, although it took a little longer. Their employees had to learn to trust the new way of interacting. Yet they loved being given honest feedback and actually demanded more of it.

For Reflection

How many times this week have you given your employees feedback?

If you were teaching a first-time manager, what would you say about giving feedback?

Do you benefit from honest feedback? How?

40

LEARN FROM THE PAST, BUT DON'T LIVE IN IT

Good or bad, yesterday is gone. Embrace the good from yesterday that will move you forward today and tomorrow and cast off the rest.

In More Depth

It is important to honor what we have gained from the past. We've learned much. We have experienced great insights and had many positive learning situations. Some of what we tried didn't work, but we profited from these experiences.

Don't keep repeating or re-creating the past. Today's world, with the people, technology, and situations in it, is in a constant state of change. To be very successful, you must use your past history as a foundation from which to decide what to do, but not be bound by it. You must apply the best of the past into the ever-changing present.

Realize that your success depends on your responding to problems and opportunities of today, with today's tools.

The Idea in Action

Paul was vice president for a carpet cleaning company. He was justifiably proud of his accomplishments and his ascent on the career ladder. However, in the last few years he felt that his job had become more difficult.

Sales had been declining, but Paul wrote that off to increased competition. Recruiting workers was more difficult, but he wrote that off to the "poor attitude of young people." The internal reporting and information systems were adequate, but he didn't get reports showing all the trends, as did Connie, his counterpart in another region. He figured he didn't have time to play with "that damned computer" the way she did.

Paul told his wife, "This job just isn't that much fun anymore."

His wife smiled. She knew he needed some honest feedback. "Honey, you resist changing with today's needs. Down at the volunteer center we have had to change. We don't get volunteers like we used to. We don't do fund raising like we used to. The manager doesn't manage like she did 15 years ago. The world is changing, Paul, and you need to jump on. Be rigorous about what works today and what needs to be changed, get rid of the outdated, and bring back the old magic that got you a vice presidency—the willingness to change, innovate, take risks, and try new things."

Paul began what he termed a "6-month revitalization project." That 6 months was the most fun Paul had had in the last 10 years. Paul, his employees, and his customers felt a renewed energy and drive.

For Reflection

What are the three best ideas from the past that still work for you today?
What are the three worst ideas from the past that you are still using today?
What stops you from leaving the past behind?

41

DON'T MAKE UNNECESSARY DECISIONS

Don't get trapped in an excessive decision-making web. Many decisions should be made by subordinates. Don't make major decisions for little problems. Unless there is a good, long-term, and important reason for you to make a decision, don't.

In More Depth

A manager can frequently get bogged down in making too many decisions. You should be making strategic decisions, long-range decisions, policy and some procedure decisions, and crisis decisions.

You do not want to make decisions that are supposed to be the province of your subordinates, especially the managers or supervisors who report to you. If you do, you will cripple their decision-making abilities. Certainly, you can collaborate with them, but only to the extent that you guide their thinking, not make the decision for them.

You must make the strategic decisions—the important ones which affect your organization's ability to perform its mission. Those decisions require careful thought and consideration. You won't have the time or energy for them if you are making the wrong kinds of decisions.

The Idea in Action

Haley was the manager of a megabookstore. Haley had graduated just 3 years earlier. She was smart, worked hard, and was well liked by her employees. When the opening came up to manage the store, the regional vice president took a chance on Haley, who showed real promise within the company.

After about 6 months, she was "worn to a frazzle." She found herself bogged down by too many decisions. Haley was not prone to rash decisions. She prided herself on carefully considering the implications of every decision, but one day she just went over her tolerance threshold when an employee asked her to decide on the color of the sign he was printing.

The employee was taken aback. He was so flustered that he just blurted out what was on his mind. "Well, you do make all the decisions around here so I thought we always had to go through you." Haley got the hint. She called her management team together and announced that from this day forward supervisors would make all decisions within their areas of responsibilities. She would be available to consult with them, but she was no longer making the decisions.

From that point on, whenever employees asked her for a decision, she referred them to an area supervisor or assistant manager. Haley was amazed at how much time she had wasted in making unnecessary decisions.

For Reflection

If you were to categorize the decisions you make into important, somewhat important, or unimportant, what percentage would be in each category?

What tips would you give another manager who tended to make unnecessary decisions?

What would happen to your organization if you made all the decisions?

42

RUN TECHNOLOGY; DON'T LET IT RUN YOU

Know technology. Stay current with and use technology, but don't let it run the organization. You are responsible for running the business. Technology is there to help you, not run you.

In More Depth

As a manager you must absolutely be aware of technology—what it can do for you and your organization as well as what technology your competition is using. You do not, however, need to be imprisoned by it.

The majority of us managers today have a limited knowledge of technology. The primary reason is that we developed our early (pre-management) careers when the use of technology was limited.

You must stay current with technology and use it to your advantage. Don't be frightened by it (yes, many of us are!). You must use it to maintain your competitive position, not only with your customers or public, but also with your employees.

You are responsible for running your business. That means exploring all the tools which may help you, your people, and your organization. Technology can be a great help to your organization. Take the upper hand and make it do for you what you want.

The Idea in Action

Felicia owned three restaurants. She wanted to expand further. Felicia, however, felt that the operation was getting out of control. She needed to find tools to help her manage.

Felicia had a conversation with a venture capitalist about franchising her operations. He told her that she had a great concept, but she couldn't do it yet because her technology was not adequate to operate a larger operation.

So she hired a technology whiz to handle all the technical matters while she focused on running the business. They did not get along well. The expert told her that she needed to do this or that—that she couldn't do this or that—and basically began to direct her business. Technology had begin to run her.

She got rid of him and over the next year became very involved in learning how the various technologies could help her. She attended seminars, took classes, talked with experts informally, went to trade shows, and watched demonstrations.

At the end of the year she again spoke with the venture capitalist. "Someday I want to explore franchising again, but for now I am going to expand on my own. Can you help me raise some money? You see, I've discovered the most incredible technology that will allow me to do what I had never dreamed."

For Reflection

Do you control technology, or does it control you?

If you were going to explore one new technology you've heard of, what would it be?

What stops you from getting more involved with your understanding and use of technology?

43
DO REALITY CHECKS

The higher you go in management, the less likely people will tell you the unvarnished truth. You are insulated in many ways—from the outside as well as within the organization. It is vital to validate your perceptions of what is going on.

In More Depth

One of the most difficult challenges facing you as a manager is to get real, clear, and truthful information. The higher you go in management, the less likely people are to give you the unedited truth. Unless you do something to get the real information, you will eventually be operating with faulty knowledge.

You must do reality checks. You must verify your perceptions of what is going on within your organization. You must also establish an openness to hearing information which you may not like to hear.

Establish an expectation for accuracy within your area of influence. When you suspect that you are being given filtered information, you can ask more probing questions or ask for some verification.

The Idea in Action

Milga was the senior editor of a major metropolitan newspaper. Milga had established a reputation for being very direct. Some of them interpreted this behavior as being angry or mean. Many of her staff members would cower in fear. They also started withholding any unpleasant information from her.

Milga did not have time to keep up on all the details of the operation. Instead, she would usually ask her editors. They would tell her, and while not lying, they would give the data a slant that they knew she would appreciate.

Milga stumbled onto facts that contradicted what her staff had told her. Usually they hadn't told her any lies, but had simply withheld information. Milga immediately began a series of reality checks. She scheduled time to talk with employees one on one. She walked through the editorial department and observed what was actually going on. She selectively read her reports to see if they aligned with the information she was being told.

She also took another smart action. She did not go back and blame her employees. Instead, she saw where the real problem lay—with her. She had to find ways to allow real, unedited information to flow to her. She set a new tone and new expectation for her staff.

They responded, although gingerly at first. It wasn't long before Milga was getting better and cleaner information than ever before. She kept on running her reality checks—to keep herself and others on track. She makes better decisions today because of it.

For Reflection

How do you conduct reality checks within your sphere of influence?

How much "editing" do you suspect is going on with the information you receive?

When was the last time you validated your most profound belief about your organization?

44

ALWAYS HAVE A BACKUP PLAN

Things will not always run perfectly. Accepting that, you can (and should) anticipate where problems may arise. That's not being negative. It's simply being prudent. Once problems are anticipated, design a backup plan to handle any emergency or crisis.

In More Depth

This may sound like a waste of time. What is a waste of time is to fumble around when your original strategy starts going off base. Assuming that your plan involves an important goal, it is imperative that you find a new way to achieve your goal. Remember, reaching the goal is what is important—not the path that gets you there. In an organization which exists to achieve some purpose, the overriding concern is to achieve that purpose. Which path you take is much less important.

There is great value in just considering a backup plan. Doing so forces a discipline, the discipline to consider alternatives. Don't be too surprised if on occasion you opt for plan B instead of your original one. Great insight comes from considering the alternatives. You may see an opportunity which had not made itself evident before. You might just like the backup plan better.

The Idea in Action

Gail was superintendent of schools. When she first went into administration she set objectives for the year. For the most part, the strategies worked. However, they sometimes failed. She would then spend hours and hours figuring out some way to "rescue" the situation. As a result, her thought processes were less than optimal.

Sue, a superintendent in another district, had become a mentor to Gail. When Gail called Sue to commiserate about a plan gone bad, Sue asked her what her backup plan was. Gail responded, "I don't have one."

"Don't have one?" Sue seemed shocked. "You always should have a backup plan."

"Why should I waste my time coming up with a backup plan?" Gail asked.

"Because you know that sometimes even the best plan will flop. It's better to think things through when you have all the information in front of you and when you are not pressured. You'll come up with a better plan. Also, you'll be in a better position to decide on the best plan," Sue advised.

Gail marveled at the obvious truth of Sue's statement. "Of course," she thought. "It only makes sense." From that point on, Gail always had a backup plan.

Gail's colleagues and constituents would marvel at her ability to "pull a rabbit from the hat" when a plan was not running well. It seemed to them that she always had a backup strategy. It was true.

For Reflection

What is your backup plan for your most important initiative?

What stories could you tell about how a backup plan pulled you through when your original plan flopped?

What excuses have you heard people come up with for not having alternative plans of action?

Creativity and Innovation

45

AVOID GROUP-THINK

Group-think is dangerous. Actually, it's a killer of ideas, of innovation, of constructive criticism and debate. It takes courage to be different, but at times it's absolutely essential.

In More Depth

When everyone in a group agrees, without participating in serious dialogue and debate to reach that agreement, you may have formed a group that actually does think alike. This is dangerous, because you'll miss something and you'll engage in something that you shouldn't. It's also possible that there is a group dynamic in play that discourages (or punishes) disagreement and constructive debate.

It takes real courage to break the grip of group-think. Someone taking the lead to break up the logjam will often get little support. Frequently, there is resistance, resentment, and outright hostility. As manager, if you notice the grip of group-think, change course immediately. The consequence of not doing so is to risk your career and your company.

The Idea in Action

Chuck was vice president of a large trust department. He chaired a committee of five who were responsible for investing in stocks, bonds, and other financial instruments. They reflected the thinking of the bank in general, in that all its members had been promoted because they usually thought and acted in "the bank's way."

Such homogeneity was valuable in aligning goals and strategies for the banking operations, but presented a potential problem. Chuck had a gnawing feeling that group-think was taking place within the investment committee. There were seldom any serious differences of opinion. Decisions were made quickly and people seemed to get along very well.

With the market rising, the group had begun to think of itself as invincible—making only great decisions. Chuck shared his concern. "I think we have fallen into the trap of thinking alike, sacrificing our analytical rigor, and risking bad decisions." To his surprise, all the members agreed and said that they were glad he had voiced something which they had not been able to identify or articulate.

They made a procedural decision that every proposed investment had to have at least one person argue against it, if for no other reason than to confirm the original decision. What they did discover was that they were more confident of their decisions, and they felt very good and proud about their process.

For Reflection

In what areas have you and your team had unanimous decisions or comfortable consensus again and again?

How do you ensure that group-think is avoided in your organization?

Is it safe for someone in your organization to disagree?

46

VALUE THE ALTERNATE OPINION

Respect and embrace the alternate opinion. It sharpens your own thinking. It forces different ways of seeing a problem or opportunity. It may be right—and it may save the day.

In More Depth

Listen when people disagree with you; there may be something very important in what they are saying. Let's hope they say it in a way that isn't disagreeable, but even then value the alternate opinion.

None of us would be so arrogant as to believe that we were always right. Yet when we're in management positions, it is easy to start believing that. We tend to fall into the trap of listening only to the "experts," or the people with the most experience, or the people we like the most, or the people who always agree with us. Instead, we need to respect and embrace the alternate opinion.

If there are no differing opinions on important matters, search them out. By listening to and engaging in a real dialogue with someone who represents an alternate opinion, you have a chance to sharpen your own thinking. You may see some value in the opposing view and choose to alter your own position. Or you may become even more firmly convinced in the efficacy of your original position. That review can be valuable in itself.

The Idea in Action

Mary was supervisor of the admissions department of a large university. Mary found herself being "directive" in her approach with her staff. Whenever one of them disagreed with her on some point, Mary immediately became defensive. After a while, people stopped disagreeing with her (publicly, at least). Yet they would complain behind her back. She did notice that morale in the section was low.

She took a management class at a local community college. One night, a guest speaker lectured on accepting and embracing alternate views and opinions. It dawned on her that she did not welcome any alternate opinions and that this might be cause for some of the discontent in her office as well as some of the inefficiencies she had noticed in her office.

Mary went back to the office determined to start valuing the alternate opinion. When she told her staff members of her "insight," they all giggled. It was no surprise to them! They were still very careful about speaking up, and Mary was afraid of this at first. Over the next year, however, both she and the employees became comfortable with hearing and expressing alternate views. Sure, there were a few rough moments in the early stages, but Mary was committed to making this work.

For Reflection

If your employees were asked, how open would they say you are to hearing alternate opinions?

Why do you think many managers don't like hearing views which are different from their own?

Can you remember a time when hearing an alternate view might have saved you from a bad mistake or helped you achieve a goal that you failed to reach?

47

ASK THE "DUMB" QUESTIONS

For want of an unasked question, knowledge dies. Knowledge is your lifeblood. There is an interesting paradox here: Dumb questions frequently open the mind to brilliant answers.

In More Depth

As managers, we need to know things and to acquire knowledge. Somehow when we become managers we are even more reluctant than normal to ask the dumb questions for fear that we will look stupid or that our employees or colleagues will lose respect for us.

Ask anyway. There is a 99 percent chance that, instead of looking stupid, you will come off as courageous and curious enough to ask questions which seem simple or obvious. Most of us have stories about how that one question opened a whole new set of opportunities, or made a muddy situation become perfectly clear. If we do not ask that one question, we risk passing up great opportunities for understanding and progressing in our business.

The Idea in Action

Lawrence headed the research team at a software development company. His was a small department, but a very progressive and successful one. There was great pressure to produce new and innovative applications.

They were working on a particularly important project and were hitting dead ends. Frustration was high. They had tried everything and still no breakthroughs in the research. The company president applied even more pressure. The team started to fight. Some members became angry; others got depressed. It was a bad situation.

Lawrence agonized over the situation. What do I do?" Lawrence felt like a bolt of lightning had struck him. "Of course," he thought, "I forgot to ask simple questions, dumb questions."

The next morning he came in and announced that on Monday all team members were to go to his home, where they would hang out with one another, asking "dumb" questions. Lawrence told them: "We are going to have fun and we are going to play this game of asking one another at least 10 dumb questions about the project and our assumptions."

They really got into it. "Why do we even need computers?" "Why can't we do it without any power source?" "What's the silliest thing we could put into the software that would delight people?" "Why does A have to come before B?" It was weird, but it broke their calcified-thinking blockage.

They came through the day with some very exciting insights. The project was completed and won a software engineering award the following year.

For Reflection

What one "dumb" question would you like to have asked today?

What do you think stops people from asking the simple questions (that could mean so much)?

How do you summon the courage to ask the dumb questions?

48
INNOVATE

Can't do it better? Eventually, someone else will. Business history is filled with cases of managers who thought that there was no way to improve the product, service, or method. Demand innovation.

In More Depth

The question is not whether there will be change, but rather how you will respond to that change. One of the best ways to respond is to embrace the fact that there is always a better way and use that attitude to make change work for you.

Whether this concept comes to you through a quality improvement program, through a response to competition, or through your own professional awareness of the need for improvement, the result is the same. Every manager in every organization needs to lead the charge to find better ways of doing things.

Yes, there is always a better way. If not today, then tomorrow, it will happen. Embrace this inevitability and lead the way.

The Idea in Action

Gwen manages a regional warehouse for a manufacturer. She runs a very efficient operation. Her team is proud of its work, and receives numerous awards.

One day Gwen was asked how her operation succeeded in continually being ranked the top warehouse in the company. She responded,

"Because we never stop improving. Last year some of the guys on the loading dock came to me and said that by using a different sealant on the packages, they could save lots of time. We looked into it, but found that there was no sealant which would do what we wanted. We found a chemist who was interested in helping us. We could have ignored that, because by the time we paid the chemist, our savings from making the change wasn't much. What it did for us, however, was keep us at top efficiency.

"Here's another example," she said. "Conventional wisdom has it that conveyor systems run best with 2-inch rollers. We challenged that thinking, jury-rigging an experimental system with 3-inch rollers. We got a much smoother movement with the boxes and we seldom have to replace bent rollers now. Sounds minor, but it reduces breakage to near zero, saves us repair time, and operates quieter, making the employees happier."

She continued: "We know that our improvements won't double the company's profits, but we also know that constantly looking for better ways keeps us sharp, adds value to our service and to the profits of the company, creates a more motivated and proud work force, makes our jobs easier, and above all makes our jobs secure."

For Reflection

How do you keep innovation alive in your organization?

What stops people in your organization from believing (or acting on) the idea that "there is always a better way?"

In a world without limitations, what three things would you improve in your organization right now?

49

SEEK UNDERSTANDING, NOT JUST INFORMATION

What you really need is to understand. When you understand something, you know what to do. Information, without understanding, does not let you know what to do.

In More Depth

The goal is understanding. When you have a true understanding of the situation or the organization in general, you will have a clear mind about what to do in nearly every situation, because you will be basing your analysis and decisions upon truth. That's a very powerful position to hold.

Understanding allows you to make more informed decisions. For example: If you understand *how* something works, you will clearly see what needs to be done to fix it. If you don't understand, you are at the mercy of your ignorance. Understanding allows you to act more appropriately and more strategically. It allows you to deal with situations surgically rather than with an ax. It lightens your stress and gives you compassion.

The Idea in Action

Phyllis was getting ready to retire as production manager for a publishing company. She was an active manager, and she had earned a reputation for being very effective. She intended to be very helpful and assist the new manager in learning the operation, which was more complicated than the one she was coming from.

The new manager, Ruth Ellen, was a bit cocky. She felt that she knew all she needed to know and didn't particularly want Phyllis's advice or insights.

Phyllis approached the vice president and told him of her disappointment in working with Ruth Ellen. "She knows the surface stuff. She has all the information, but she doesn't *understand*. I have spent years going deeper into the operation, understanding why it works the way it does. I know the connections to other parts of our company system. I know how each action affects others. I understand what makes our employees tick, and I know their quirks. All this understanding makes the operation go smoothly and with maximum productivity."

Phyllis continued: "Yes, I know the textbook models for operations management, but it was my dedication to *understanding* my operation and my people from a very core level that made this facility into the model it is."

The vice president smiled at his friend of many years. "Unfortunately, not every manager cares enough to do the detective work needed to really understand an organization. You're the exception—and exceptional—not the norm."

For Reflection

How would you coach new managers to "understand" your organization?
What steps do you take to understand your area of responsibility?
Can you give an example in your career of when understanding *was much more important than* information?

50

IF IT DOESN'T WORK ONE WAY, TRY ANOTHER

Be open to different possibilities. Seldom is there just one way to do something—or one way that anything must turn out. There can be many paths to success. In fact, you may come to find that "today's failure" opens you to new ways that become tomorrow's successes.

In More Depth

This is one of the fundamental rules of life, as well as management. When something isn't going right, change the path. Find one that *does* work. If your plan isn't turning out the way you wanted, change something in the plan or change something in the implementation. If your interaction with an employee is not working out well, change the way you interact.

The key point here is to try one way, then another, then still another until you find what works. There are many paths to success. Sometimes it turns out that a failure can open the door to success, because that failure forces you to try something new!

The Idea in Action

Judy was general manager of a payroll processing company. She was a perfectionist and her weakness was her reaction when plans did not work out. All of this caused her to go into a tailspin of anxiety and anger. Her response was to redouble her efforts using her original strategy. More often than not, the same problems occurred despite added attention, effort, and money.

One day she was playing with her son, who was building a sand castle. When she tried to tell him to do it a certain way, he just looked at her and said, "I like my way better." Sure enough, his sand castle turned out just fine. Because Judy wasn't particularly proficient at building sand castles, hers fell down halfway through its building. So she started again. Her son looked at her and began giggling. "What's wrong?" she demanded. He continued giggling. "It's going to fall down again." She asked, "Why?" To which he responded, "You're doing the same thing over again. You have to do it a different way."

His wisdom hit her like a lightning bolt. She thought to herself, "That is exactly what is happening at the job. Whenever something doesn't work, I go right back and do it again. How stupid can I be?"

She went back into work on Monday determined not to repeat the same mistakes. When something didn't go well, she asked some of her staff, "What could we try to do differently?" After they recovered from their shock, they gave her several alternatives, one of which was a clear winner.

For Reflection

Thinking over the last two weeks, when did you try something different when a routine didn't work?

What might you do differently with one of the employees who causes you the most grief?

How could you remind yourself to be open to new possibilities when the first one doesn't turn out well?

51

LOOK RIGHT IN FRONT OF YOU

Too often, we forget to look at what is "staring us in the face." Sometimes we look for deep meanings or hidden information, only to discover that it is right in front of us all the time. Consider what may be too obvious to notice.

In More Depth

As a management discipline, look right in front of you. See the obvious. Use your "street smarts" instead of the philosophical, theoretical, and complex methods you have been educated in and taught to use.

In-depth analysis and searching for deep, and sometimes hidden, meanings can be a valuable exercise. So can asking yourself, "What is obvious here? What have I missed because I walked by the obvious?"

To see the obvious, you need to slow down. You need to step back to see what is directly in front of you. When you shift your mindset to a different perspective, you can see what you have been walking by for so long. It's like a wonderful discovery. You can see very clearly what step you should take in order to achieve your goal.

The Idea in Action

Richard had established a reputation throughout the computer industry: Richard the Wise Man. He had earned this reputation not because he was a salesman who sold components to various computer companies, but because he could go into a company and see the obvious. He had become friendly with managers in these companies who came to rely on this counsel and advice.

On one occasion, Richard met the owner of a small, but fast-growing computer company for lunch. The owner asked Richard what he thought the problem was with the company's new product. (It had not been selling well.) "Well," started Richard, "you made the keyboard too small. People can't use it comfortably."

The owner's jaw dropped. "Do you mean to tell me that we spent millions developing this new computer and it's the keyboard that is our problem?"

Richard smiled. "Yep."

The owner saw the obvious (after having it pointed out to him). From that point on, and at every monthly executive meeting, his agenda included this item: "The Obvious Things That We Are Missing." The staff doesn't leave that item until they have come up with at least one major obvious point. The procedure has saved the company much anguish and made it a lot of money.

The owner sent Richard the plaque which started Richard's reputation. It read: "To Richard the Wise Man." Others have benefited from Richard's ability to look right in front of him and to see the obvious.

For Reflection

What is one issue that is right in front of you which you hadn't noticed before now?

How can you discipline yourself to see the obvious?

What stops you from seeing the obvious? What excuses have you invented (too busy, more important things to do, and so on)?

Getting the Big Picture

52

SEE YOUR BUSINESS FROM THE CUSTOMER'S POINT OF VIEW

The customer is the only reason your organization exists. Without customers, you and your organization has no purpose. See it from their point of view, then act on that.

In More Depth

Organizations are created to serve people. Whether we call them clients, patients, members, the public, or customers, the key point to remember is that the organization exists to serve.

To serve our "customers" well, we need to look at our organization from their point of view. We need to see what customers want and need. Then, we need to see *how, when, and where* they want and need it. If we forget to serve these people, our organization will cease to have any legitimate purpose.

When we do look and act from the customer's point of view, dramatic and wonderful things begin to happen. We get more business and more support. It's a very simple equation. If we don't, the competition will.

The Idea in Action

Damien was a library administrator. He decided to conduct a survey of how well the libraries were serving the public. He expected to receive many accolades from the public and was going to use the results to kick off a round of employee acknowledgments. Instead he got a shock. Twenty-eight percent of the public was dissatisfied with the service. Another 37 percent gave the service only a "passing" grade. Only 35 percent of the public thought that the libraries were doing a fine job. He was shocked and concerned.

He knew that he would have to respond, yet he was afraid. "This means a big change," he thought. He knew that he was going to have to lead the effort to see things from the public's point of view. He conducted focus groups to get more insight and information. He also asked each employee to talk with five patrons during the month and ask what the library was doing well and what it could do better.

Damien was concerned that the employees would resent the survey work. Again, he was surprised. The employees wanted to do good work; they wanted happy library patrons and they wanted to be proud of their organization.

Over the next year, Damien and his group—The Great Libraries Task Force—poured through hundreds of suggestions and then acted on the information.

The result? His library system was featured as a model of a great library system. Happier employees. Happier patrons. More successful fund raising. A better system. And lots and lots of personal and professional satisfaction.

For Reflection

How do you know what your "customers" want and need?

What have you and your organization done this year to respond to customer desires?

What stops your organization from being more responsive to the customers?

53

BE SOCIALLY RESPONSIBLE

Your organization is part of the community. This is good business. As with a garden: to reap you must sow.

In More Depth

We need to realize that we are part of a greater community. We take from this community: its people, its physical resources, its attention, and its energy. Nearly always we rely on our community for our customers, clients, patients, or members. Because we take from the community, we must replace some of what we have taken.

It's tempting to fall into the trap of thinking that since you pay your employees and pay your taxes, there is nothing more that needs to be done. Not true. Being socially responsible does not mean that you have to give all your profits away or that you have to spend all your time doing community volunteer work. It does mean that you see yourself and your organization as an active and participating member of the community.

The Idea in Action

Alice was general manager of a small clothing manufacturer. Alice was concerned about making a profit. She knew that without profits, no one would have a job, and there would be no company. She carried it a bit too far, though, by always trying to find ways to "take advantage" of the city, of employees, of the neighborhood.

Over the years, the company developed a reputation as being a difficult place to work, totally "out for itself," and a poor community citizen. Alice noticed that she was having trouble with city hall whenever the company needed some planning and zoning help. She also noticed that once the employees got some training, they would often go to work for competitors that were more socially responsible. Finally, she noticed that other businesses were getting great press coverage for some of the community-minded things they were doing.

Alice didn't like feeling pressured to be socially responsible. However, she realized that from a business sense, she needed to be more socially responsible. She talked with people in the neighborhood before constructing new buildings. She personally volunteered to sit on the community standards board for manufacturing ethics. She encouraged employees to volunteer for community causes by giving them a paid 2-hour leave every week to do so.

Alice finally realized that as an organization you are part of a larger community.

For Reflection

In what ways are you and your organization socially responsible?

What excuses does your organization use to avoid social responsibility?

What two socially responsible endeavors could you initiate that would be responsible both to the community and to the successful operation of your organization?

54

THE SOUND YOU HEAR IN THE DISTANCE IS YOUR COMPETITION COMING

Competition keeps you sharp. You improve—or you fade away. Every day, imagine that your best and most fierce competitor planned to make a major move in your arena. Then run your operation with that focus and intensity.

In More Depth

Competition is fun. It sharpens thinking and action. It provides focus and attention. It brings passion and interest. Nearly always, it makes both sides better.

As most players will admit, however, it is much more fun to win. In some situations, it is vital to win. It would be nice to believe that we all live in a harmonious and collaborative world where nobody could lose. That simply isn't the case. Sometimes organizations that do not respond to and beat the competition go out of business, and people lose their jobs

When you run your organization in a manner that focuses your energy and resources on the goal while remaining very aware of the current or potential competition, you will move closer to the goal.

The Idea in Action

Rowena had been marketing director of a home health-care provider for 6 years. She knew her job, company, and industry well, but she was becoming bored. It showed in her work. For example, she led the yearly planning project. The team copied last year's plan and then took time off for golf.

Sales increased primarily because demand for home care had increased and not because of anything Rowena had done. Down the street, the smaller corporate competitor had started a new and innovative delivery service and several of the little mom-and-pops had expanded their offerings.

Next year the project planning team did exactly the same thing, not thinking that the competition was gaining on them. The smaller corporation ran an "all-out" marketing effort, and three of the mom-and-pops formed a consortium that produced some unique and valuable synergies. Sales actually declined for Rowena's company.

Rowena and her team panicked. They had to act in response to real competition. This time the team formulated a great marketing plan. However, her competitors didn't focus on her company; rather they focused on the greater target and came up with even more innovative marketing strategies. Rowena and her team now operate as if they are always facing their fiercest competitor. It keeps them alert and motivated.

For Reflection

What strategies did you adopt this year as a result of actual or potential competition?

How do you and your team keep an eye on the target, while responding to competition?

What are five strategies the competition is using which you aren't?

55

BE AWARE OF SYMBOLIC VALUE

People are always looking for clues to other people's intentions. Symbols serve that purpose. Be aware of what message you are sending. Nearly everything you do has symbolic value. People will interpret symbols as intention.

In More Depth

As a manager you are set apart from your employees. As such, you must be aware of the symbolic value of your position. Nearly everything you do will be interpreted. Employees will interpret your behaviors, style, quirks, decisions, announcements, absences, attendance, glances, silence, who you're with, when you're gone. It is a natural part of our lives especially our organizational and management lives.

Do be aware of interpretation and act accordingly. As managers, we know that we are fallible human beings who sometimes forget things, have bad moods, and say things which we do not interpret as any more than general conversation.

In your management, be aware (and beware) of symbols. Consider what message you are sending. Use it to your advantage and use it appropriately.

The Idea in Action

Terry had come from the ranches of Oklahoma to become the president of a consumer electronics company. He was a brilliant and shrewd businessman who understood the power of symbols.

He knew that his employees would be watching him so he took advantage of that. He made sure he was in the office early and left late. He publicly rewarded people when they did outstanding jobs. He would give medals, awards, and trophies which were displayed by their recipients. More symbolism.

As he worked his way up through the ranks, Terry carefully groomed his symbolic persona. He cultivated the symbolism of being honest, hardworking, nonthreatening (and to some of his competitors nonchallenging—a big misinterpretation on their part). He had his office decorated with success-oriented images—photos of people he admired, motivational sayings, and awards.

When he was promoted to president, he knew that a symbol was worth more than 20 memos so he announced that if the employees met a certain corporate objective he would personally say thank you to every person in the company. They reached that goal, which was significant. He lived up to his promise and spent the next week shaking every single employee's hand in the company—all 1845 of them at five different sites.

To some, that would seem like a wasted week. Hardly. Terry knew the symbolic power of his actions. Want to guess whether they made their goals the next year?

For Reflection

What are three actions which you take to send a message to your employees?

What is one action or behavior which you are now engaged in which could be misinterpreted?

How could you use the power of symbols to help your organization?

56
ACCEPT RISK

You cannot eliminate risk. Learn to live with it. You can reduce risk by understanding, learning, planning, and testing—but there is always some risk. Embrace it. Let it motivate you.

In More Depth

Risk is part of your life as a manager. You must make decisions and act on your best judgments. That means that you will not always have all the information you want. Thus, there is the risk of failure. Hopefully, the probabilities are in your favor, but there is still a risk.

You cannot eliminate risk. It is a part of your life. Given that, it is wise to learn to live with it. When you accept risk as a given, it no longer causes as much fear or apprehension.

If you accept risk, or if you're even more progressive and actually embrace risk, you can use it to motivate you. Knowing that there is some inherent danger (risk), you will be more sharp. You'll take the extra steps in preparing.

Whether you hate the thought of risk, or whether you love the excitement it gives you, remember this: You cannot eliminate risk. Make it work for you. Use it to your advantage. Embrace it as a potential friend.

The Idea in Action

Janet had a fear of taking risks. She was a retail department supervisor just starting out in her management career. She avoided every risk that she could. She was fairly creative about doing so. When a decision which looked risky, she would go to her boss and ask her what to do. Her boss didn't catch on and made the decisions for Janet, who then felt she had eliminated the risk.

At other times, Janet would obsess about little decisions which had a small element of risk. For example, she needed to decide how many desk sets they should order for the fall season. This was a simple decision, but she spent 2 days going back through the records of the past 2 years to see the trend in desk set sales.

Her fear of risk was getting out of hand. Finally, her manager saw what was going on and asked Janet to lunch. Her manager said, "Janet, you cannot eliminate all risk. You have to accept some of that as a manager. I expect that you will make some mistakes. People, situations, the economy, styles make for a hopelessly complex equation. You can do only your best and accept the risks that come along with it."

Janet took the advice to heart, although it was a long time before she felt comfortable. Today, Janet makes big decisions as the lead buyer for her company and lets that risk motivate instead of stop her.

For Reflection

In what areas of your work do you accept risk?

In what areas do you avoid risk?

What can you do to make the inherent risk of managing an organization work in your favor?

57

THERE IS NO SUCH THING AS JOB SECURITY

Job security comes from inside you, not from rules, policies, or legal prece-dents. Keep up to date, learn, and perform well. Become very valuable to your profession, your company, and your industry. Constantly strive to provide value to your organization—that's your best security.

In More Depth

Job security is an "inside" job. It is inside because your best job securi-ty is to be so valuable to your organization that it cannot possibly get rid of you. Or you can become so valuable to competitors as well that your own organization will do everything possible to keep you. That is real job security.

The people who have the most job security are those who are most up to date in their field and those who perform the best. They learn. They study. They improve and add to their skills. They don't just repeat the same work over and over; they constantly look for ways to improve themselves and their work. They also become involved with their field professionally. They get to know other people in the indus-try and in their field. You and your organization will certainly benefit.

The Idea in Action

Sheila was a marketing manager for a national syndicate of newspa-pers. She knew that the industry was one that seemed to always be in a state of flux. There were mergers, economic downturns, and the simple capricious nature of publishers.

Sheila was a very "street smart" professional and she knew that her job security lay in her ability to produce, her knowledge of the job, and her contacts.

She was constantly learning new aspects of the job. She read voraciously about marketing, sales, advertising, business, psychology, and sociology. Thus, she and her people were always using the most up-to-date information available. Their effort translated into higher and more profitable sales. She knew that this was her security. She joined professional organizations, attended conventions and trade shows, and subscribed to the industry publications. She worked her contacts.

An observer might think that Sheila was obsessed with finding another job. That was not the case. In fact, she has had only two jobs in the past 18 years. Rather, she has job security—job security from the "inside."

She admits, "It takes a lot of work to get this 'job security,' but it's what I would do anyway. I want to learn. I want to be a top performer. I want me and my people to have the latest and best information. I want us to be well connected and have access to people. It's just good business."

For Reflection

How do you keep up to date in your career?

What could you do to develop more "internal" job security?

What do you do that makes you so valuable that your organization would always want you around?

Managers Are
Human, Too

58

MOOD IMPACTS MANAGEMENT

Your mood changes your management. Good decisions are made when you are in a positive frame of mind. We all have moods. The key is to make the most of good ones, and to avoid doing damage during bad ones.

In More Depth

We all have our moods. Some days we're happy and everything goes well. Other days we are grouchy and sad. That's part of being human. The key to successful management is to realize that your mood affects your management. Granted, you cannot wait for a good mood to happen before you manage, no more than you can avoid managing when you're in a bad mood. Again, the key is to *realize* that there is an impact and to make the appropriate modifications.

This is tougher than it sounds. It requires a good self-awareness. Then it requires the discipline to be honest with ourselves and act on it.

Remember: Be aware of your moods and the way they impact your management and adjust accordingly.

The Idea in Action

Rusty was the nursing manager of an inner-city hospital. Rusty liked to believe that he was always in control—of himself and of every situation. He prided himself on staying calm and his ability to handle stress.

However, Rusty found himself in a new and very uncomfortable situation. His father was gravely ill and Rusty started going through some dramatic mood swings. Some days he would be very stressed and would bark at people, hastily call meetings, and make decisions off the top of his head—all of this in an attempt to avoid stress and the painful feelings of his father's illness. Other days, he would be in a great mood. His mind was clearer and his interactions with people were much better.

A friend and trusted confidante took him aside: "It's perfectly natural what you're feeling about your father, but you've got to be careful about how it impacts your management. Don't call brainstorming meetings when you are in such a bad mood. No one feels creative when you're that way. People reflect your mood. And when you're feeling great, enjoy it. But also make some of your tough decisions then, when your mind is clearer and you have the energy to tackle them."

Rusty trusted the friend and knew that she was right. He took her advice and lightened up on himself and others when he was in a bad mood and he pushed himself a little more when he was in a great mood so as to take full advantage of the feeling.

For Reflection

When you're in a great mood, how would you describe your management style?

Alternately, when you're in a bad mood, how would you describe your style?

How do you stay aware of your mood?

59

CONQUER YOUR EGO

Know your ego. Don't be controlled by it. Self-confidence is important. Self-aggrandizement and inflated self-importance are an Achilles' heel.

In More Depth

We all have an ego. When it is healthy, this shows up as self-confidence. That is a very valuable attribute to have as a manager. You will also want to be proud of yourself. That's good, too. The problem comes when you go over the line into self-aggrandizement and inflated self-importance. Most strengths, when overdone, become weaknesses.

If you recognize that success is a totality of your talent and effort, combined with the talent and effort of your team, combined with fortuitous external forces, you will maintain a healthy sense of reality.

So, know yourself and know your ego. Keep the good parts; get rid of the bad. Don't let it control you or seduce you into trusting an illusion. Use it to motivate and support you, not to devour you and block your path.

The Idea in Action

Jose enjoyed the many accolades which came to him for being the "marketing genius" behind a fast-growing department store chain. He was smart, had a great personality, and was driven. He experienced great success early in his career. He was also lucky, because the department store had a special niche which had no competition early in its development.

Jose loved the attention. A well-known business magazine picked up the human interest angle and wrote about him. He was being made into a god by the business community and by the public.

Along the way, the company experienced growing pains. Top talent left. Competition came at them from all sides. To make matters worse, the general economy slowed down. Sales for the company declined. The company and Jose's reputation were at risk. Jose was angry and embarrassed.

Jose had to face the tough reality. He had let his ego get the better of him. He was good at his work, creative, and perhaps even a genius. Yet he had let himself and others fall for the inflated illusion. He sat straight up and vowed to just be himself, and not let the ego's reign continue. He even acknowledged his own limitations when the press interviewed him for follow-up stories.

Because of his self-confidence, pride, and newfound humility, he gained many admirers and supporters. Jose receives much more *real* praise today than ever before.

For Reflection

When was the last time your ego got the better of you?
When do you think self-confidence turns into inflated self-importance?
How do you feel about colleagues who think too much of themselves?

60
BUILD IN DOWNTIME

As with a bank account, we cannot only make withdrawals on our lives. We must make some deposits as well. Rest fills the account. Renewing activities fill the account. A little each day and a big deposit occasionally will make you (your life) rich.

In More Depth

In order to perform at our peak capacity, we need to have healthy bodies and minds. We wouldn't think of not oiling our machinery or having updated, top-performing software, yet we often ignore ourselves. We run our "machinery" beyond its optimal operating capacity. Managers are human too.

Physically, we need rest and play, as well as work. Emotionally, we need the time and willingness to connect with ourselves and other people. Spiritually, we need time to connect with our higher power, nature, and our own inner wisdom. To do this, we must build in some downtime or else. It might also be called unfocused time.

So much of our life requires intense focus. It is important to create downtime that does not require anything of you. Empty your mind, stop thinking for a while. You will be that much sharper, alert, creative, and focused when you need to be.

The Idea in Action

B.A. (Bob Andrew) always worked hard. He studied hard, spent long hours after being recruited by a prominent law firm, abandoned vacations so he could work on extra "important" cases, and came in early and stayed late after being made a managing partner.

He had a great house and lots of money. His home life was a little shaky, but he provided for his family well. He was respected in the community, although he had a only few "real" friends with whom he could sincerely laugh and share his feelings.

One day, B.A. was working at the office when he started having chest pains. Fortunately, the janitor was there and called the ambulance.

The mild heart attack was a warning. Out of the hospital, he took his doctor's advice and began a regular exercise program. He reignited the passion between him and his wife primarily by taking time with her and communicating once again. He blocked every Friday afternoon off his calendar. That was his time to reexplore his buried creativity. He had breakfast once every 2 weeks with his "best buddy" from college, a person with whom he felt very comfortable and he could be himself completely.

B.A. had to learn the hard way to build in some downtime. Learn the easy way. Take some time. Make it a priority. Engage in wonderfully renewing activities.

For Reflection

What stops you from building in some downtime?
When is the best time for you to rest?
What is the most positive action you could take this week to rest or renew yourself?

61

SEE AND FEEL YOURSELF AS A LEADER

You need to build your internal image to reflect the role of the leader. In order to be an effective leader, you must see and feel yourself as being a leader.

In More Depth

In the early stages, you can "fake it" until you make it. However, eventually you will need to experience yourself as being a leader. If you do not, you will project that image to your people.

We all carry mental baggage—self-images which may not be positive. First, you need to develop some awareness of how you really see yourself, and how this manifests in your life. Once you know what you're dealing with, decide how you want to be seen. You start to listen to that little inner voice guiding you. Replace self-defeating and low self-esteem thoughts with positive ones.

Another technique is called imaging. Just imagine yourself as being a successful leader. How do you act? How do you think as leader? Then when the real situation comes, you have already had a trial run at it.

The Idea in Action

Linda was just elected to the presidency of the local PTA. She had great interest in the organization and great commitment to see it succeed. However, she never saw herself as a leader.

She saw herself as a good employee at the local telephone company; a good mother; and a good neighbor and volunteer. But leader?! That was another story. Linda decided to rise to the occasion and embark on a self-development program to benefit the organization and benefit her personally.

First she realized that she would be making presentations to various groups. She decided to invest in some professional clothing and went to an image consultant to see if anything would be beneficial in developing her professional appearance. She joined a Toastmasters' group to develop her presentation skills.

Then she took the time to explore her inner feelings about being a leader. She realized that she had been taught that "nice little girls don't want attention." (Nowhere did she learn that she might be a leader.) She developed three short, positive statements which she kept repeating to herself: "I am a leader, people want me to lead." "I believe in myself." "I project confidence."

She also had fun imagining herself in leadership situations, playing out various scenarios until she arrived at one in which she felt comfortable and successful. It was amazing to her to see how comfortable she was when the real situations presented themselves.

For Reflection

What does a leader look and feel like? Do you feel this way?

What are you doing outwardly to present yourself as a leader?

What are you doing inwardly to develop a leadership attitude, and how much time have you spent daydreaming lately?

62
DON'T GET LAZY

Success can foster laziness. Don't get trapped here. Evaluate your own performance. Better yet, have other people evaluate your performance and give you honest feedback. If you need a rest, rest. If you're bored, get out, change jobs, or revitalize your job and get back on track.

In More Depth

Success is wonderful. Most managers have worked very hard to earn their success and justifiably have a right to be proud and to enjoy the rewards of their labor. Sometimes, however, a danger lurks in this success. Occasionally, the successful manager becomes lazy.

Enjoy the rewards, but don't' get lazy. Find some project that intrigues you and install an operational manager or structure beneath you so that you can do what you find interesting while still guiding the ship. Or set a new and challenging goal so that you can get your passion back.

Find ways to energize your career and your life. Avoid the laziness trap. Enjoy your rewards, but enjoy them in such a way that your organization also benefits. You're the leader. The organization needs your interest, attention, and passion.

The Idea in Action

Gary was vice president of sales for a multinational construction firm.

It was in large measure through his efforts that the firm had grown and prospered.

Gary noticed that he was becoming less interested in going to work every morning. He would go in a little late, leisurely read his mail, call a friend to join him for lunch, and focus on trivia. When a problem arose, he would refer it to one of the sales managers. When a new project required a lot of work and input, he would ask a committee to formulate the project. In a nutshell, Gary had become lazy on the job.

He talked about it with his wife one night. Doris smiled knowingly. She said, "Gary, you haven't taken a real vacation in years. The work has become routine and you have developed other interests. You're a good manager and a brilliant salesman. You always loved sales and you haven't been out on a sales call in over 3 years. You aren't lazy. You're tired and bored. So do what the Gary I married would do. He'd find some way to have fun at what he was doing and then he would throw his heart into it."

Gary announced that he was taking a 3-month trip around the world with Doris. He put his management team in charge and said that he would not be available, but that he would return and once again take this firm to new heights (and he meant it). Over the next year he found ways to renew himself and his commitment to the job.

For Reflection

Have you ever seen a successful manager who became lazy? What happened?

How do you avoid becoming lazy?

What do you think is the real reason successful managers become lazy?

63

USE DRUGS AND LOSE

Abusing drugs and alcohol will destroy you and potentially your organization. Management and leadership demand your full attention. You cannot manage and lead well when you're in a fog.

In More Depth

You need your full faculties in order to be a superior manager. Abusing drugs and alcohol will take that away. More than that, it will destroy your career. If you abuse drugs, you lose.

Management is filled with pressure. We all want to release the tension and stress that build with the job. Do that, but don't do it with drugs and alcohol. It should be obvious that we're not talking about the glass of wine at dinner or the beer while watching the game. The problem is when the booze or pills become a crutch to get you through. That's abuse.

Abuse drugs and you lose. Your organization loses. The people around you lose. Winning is better, even if it does take a little discipline and work.

The Idea in Action

Bert was regional manager for a group of banks. He was smart. He worked hard. He had a great personality. As he progressed through the corporate ranks, he found that the stress was building. Also, he was expected to be more social for professional reasons.

Bert had started drinking in high school, and increasing it while he was in a fraternity at college. He had also experimented with drugs, yet never really became too involved with them. Bert would relieve stress by having a beer after work. Then it got to the point where he would go home after having the beer and have a cocktail to unwind. As he entertained more, he felt that he functioned much better after drinks.

After a while, two drinks became three and then four. He'd occasionally try a line of cocaine and that would make his behavior erratic. He noticed that people were turning down his invitations to lunch and an "afterwork drink."

Bert's drinking got worse until it could be ignored no longer. The vice president confronted Bert, "You're a great banker, and I would love to see you continue your career with us, but this behavior is stopping as of now. It's your choice what to do about it. We have an employee assistance program for people who are having a problem with drugs or alcohol...."

Bert was lucky. He didn't have to lose his job. He did enter a treatment center and became a clean and sober man.

For Reflection

Who in your organization abuses drugs or alcohol?

How do you relieve your stress?

What would you do if someone who worked for you had a drinking problem? What advice would you give?

64
SMILE

Smile and the organization smiles with you. Smiling suggests confidence, camaraderie, and success.

In More Depth

Your job is to lead and manage. This requires your interaction with people. By smiling you create a relationship with people. People work much harder for people they like.

Superior leaders create relationships with their people on the basis of mutual respect and a genuine concern for others' welfare. You can say you respect and care for people, but we submit that if you never smile at them, they will not "read" it that way. They will assume you're just mouthing the words and being hypocritical.

Obviously you do not go around smiling all the time. Just be natural. Smile when it's appropriate and don't smile when it's inappropriate—but if you're not used to doing it, make an extra effort for a week or two and see what happens. You can get results without smiling, but you will not achieve a significant improvement over the long term. Good employees go where they are appreciated and liked.

The Idea in Action

Samantha had just landed a job as manager of a medical products firm. She was aware that she would need to command respect and establish control.

She decided that she needed to project a tough image, especially since she was a woman and the majority of her staff were men. However, the staff referred to her (behind her back) as the Iron Lady of XYZ. She always had a set jaw and determined look. People were not comfortable with her stern appearance, which had a negative impact on teamwork and interaction.

She heard rumors that several of her top people were exploring other jobs. While "the job was getting done," morale was low.

Samantha went to a trusted friend for advice: "What should I do?" He said, "You're very competent. However, people don't feel that you like them much. Your perpetually stern look scares people. All you have to do is *smile*. I believe that you really do care, but you don't show it. They need to see that you are pleased; otherwise, they wonder what is wrong."

Sam did begin to smile more. It was awkward at first and she felt uncomfortable. However, the results were so positive (people smiling back and being more relaxed, happier, friendlier, more cooperative, and more fun) that she kept at it. She also noticed that *she* was getting more enjoyment from her job.

For Reflection

How often do you smile? Have you smiled at work today? (Don't forget at home, too!)

Have you shown your employees that you like them?

What is your face saying?